MW01259651

INDUCTIVE STUDY CURRICULUM
STUDENT GUIDE

OLD TESTAMENT/*Character Study*

ABRAHAM
A Journey of Faith

Abraham
INDUCTIVE STUDY CURRICULUM

Unless otherwise noted, all Scripture quotations are from the New American
Standard Bible, ©1960, 1962, 1963, 1968, 1971, 1972, 1973, 1975, 1977, 1995
by the Lockman Foundation, and are used by permission.

Enrichment word definitions are taken with permission from
Merriam-Webster, Inc. Merriam-Webster's Collegiate Dictionary. 10th ed.
Springfield, Mass., U.S.A.: Merriam-Webster, 1996, c1993.

Precept, Precept Ministries International, Precept Ministries International
The Inductive Bible Study People, the Plumb Bob design, Precept Upon Precept,
and In & Out are trademarks of Precept Ministries International.

1st edition
Printed in the United States of America

TABLE OF CONTENTS

Abraham

INTRODUCTION TO INDUCTIVE STUDY

Abraham

1. Inductive Bible Study - _____

2. There are _____ of Inductive Bible Study:

    a. _____ - _____ ?

    b. _____ - _____ ?

    c. _____ - _____ ?

3. Tools of Observation

    a. The _____ questions

Abraham

　　b. Mark _____ and _____

　　c. Make _____

4. Tools of Interpretation

　　a. _____

　　　_____! It rules interpretation.

　　b. _____

　　c. _____

5. Application

a. _____   - resulting in

_____   _____

First Step of Faith

Do you look at other people and wonder why they are so unique and you are so... **ordinary**? They are talented, beautiful, smart, and funny and you... well, you're just awkward, insecure, and unremarkable. Guess what? Everybody feels ordinary sometimes! The truth is that someone *will* always be more talented, more beautiful, smarter, or funnier than you. This can sound depressing but not if you know God and the story of His friend Abraham.

> You will discover how one small step of faith can become a gigantic leap when you follow God.

Abraham was ordinary, but through God's promise, his life became **extraordinary**. God used Abraham's faith in Him to impact every nation and generation on earth – including YOU!

And even more amazing... Abraham isn't the only one God can take from ordinary to extraordinary! He can do it with you too! All He's looking for is someone who listens to what He says, believes Him, and then moves forward, one step at a time.

As you work through this study, you will go on a journey – a journey of faith. You will discover how one small step of faith can become gigantic leaps when you follow God. Like Abraham, you can be "a friend of God" – a friend of the Creator of heaven and earth! It will take work and time to discover these things, but IT WILL BE WORTH IT! Be diligent in your study. Put down some of the demands on your time and carefully examine God's Word. Most importantly, allow the Holy Spirit to lead you into all truth. You'll be awed at what you learn and the difference it will make in your life.

Don't let truth go in one ear and out the other! Practice what you learn and you too can be a man or woman of faith who changes the world for God's glory!

Begin this journey by asking God to guide you. The prayer below is an example for you to get started.

> *Father, I ask for Your help because You are God and nothing is impossible for You. You know my schedule, the pressures and pulls of my life. You know that it is sometimes difficult for me to set aside time to study and learn about You and Your ways.*
>
> *Father, I need Your wisdom, encouragement, strength, and direction. I need confidence to face life with all its twists, turns, and difficulties. I know all this comes only from You as a gift of grace. Please create in me the desire to know Your Word and help me take time to study effectively. Meet with me in personal and intimate ways – ways that equip and sustain me for all the future holds, ways that rebuke me or restrain me if I am going the wrong way, believing something untrue. Let my heart's desire, dear Lord, please You in every way. If I am off that path, I trust You will turn me about through Your Word and by Your Spirit given to me through the New Covenant.*
>
> *I pledge to You my faithfulness to give this study all that I can, and ask You to change me as I choose the thing I need most– a real and intimate relationship with You.*
>
> *In faith, I thank You for what You are going to do as I do my part. I pray this in the name of the One who is the Way, the Truth, and the Life, Jesus Christ.*

ONE ON ONE:

Now, take a moment to write out a prayer of your own. Express to God anything specific you hope to discover about Him or yourself as you study Abraham's life. At the end of the study, look back at this prayer and record how God answered.

LESSON ONE

Before you study a book or passage in the Bible, it's important to establish context to help you to understand it. This will ensure you don't misinterpret or misunderstand events or messages God recorded. So you will begin your study of Abraham by looking at the context, which is Genesis – the book that contains his story.

> **Context** is the setting in which something is found. Look at what comes before and after a Scripture to determine how it fits into the chapter, book, and whole Bible.

Identifying key repeated words or phrases will also help you understand how his story fits in Genesis. Your first assignment is to identify and examine a key repeated phrase in Genesis.

The key repeated phrase used throughout the book of Genesis is "These are the records of the generations of _____." The phrase is first used is in Genesis 2:4, but it's difficult to recognize in the New American Standard Bible – the translation used in Inductive Study Curriculum courses. The marginal reference in the NASB is explained in the pull-out box.

The phrase is then repeated in Genesis 5:1; 6:9; 10:1; 11:10; and 11:27.

> Genesis 2:4 – This is *the account of the heavens and the earth* when they were created, in the day that the Lord God made earth and heaven.
>
> It can be translated: *These are the generations of the heavens and the earth* when they were created, in the day the Lord God made earth and heaven.

1. Look at Genesis 5:1; 6:9; 10:1; 11:10; and 11:27. Underline the phrase, "These are the generations of _____," in a distinctive way in your Bible. Then write whose generations are recorded in these verses in each of the puzzle pieces below.

Now, look at your Observation Worksheet for Genesis 11:24-32. Underline the same phrase in verse 27 and fill in the last puzzle piece.

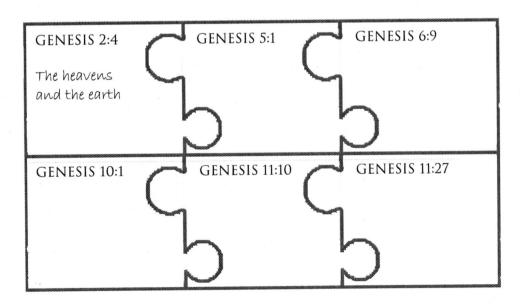

You've just determined where Abraham fits into the book of Genesis. Now you know who his **ancestors** are and what events took place before he was born. You know more from this simple exercise than many people who have been in church for decades. All it takes for anyone to understand the Bible is a little time and effort! Good job!

2. Now observe Genesis 11:24-32 by reading it and marking every occurrence of *Abram* with a blue box. (By the way, Abram's name will be changed to Abraham later.)

> **Observation** Is looking at what the text says. First, read it. Then use observation tools like marking main people in the text to help you slow down and focus on what the text says about them.

3. Using a 3x5 notecard, create a bookmark of key words and symbols you have used already. You will add to the card any new key words you discover in the course of the study.

EXAMPLE:

Abram

4. Now re-read Genesis 11:24-32 and record the names of Terah's children and their spouses and children on the chart "Abraham's Family Tree," located in the Appendix.

LESSON TWO

1. You know *what* Abram did in Genesis 11, now it's time to find out *why* he did it. Look at the following cross-references for insight into why Abram moved from Ur of the Chaldeans. (Sometimes God doesn't give all the facts at once; instead He reveals certain specifics in other books of the Bible – this is called progressive revelation.)

> **Cross-references** are other places in Scripture that give more information about the passage you are observing. Looking at what the whole counsel of God's Word has to say on a topic helps you interpret the passage more accurately.

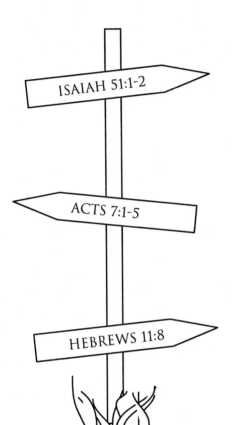

a. God is speaking to the nation of Israel in this passage. Record what He says about Abram's status when He called him.

b. Record what you learn from reading these verses.

c. Note what you learn about Abram and his journey.

2. Look at the two maps located in the Appendix. The first map is a large-scale map of the countries and cities mentioned in Genesis 11 and 12. The second map is a smaller-scale map that gives a closer view of Canaan. Starting at Ur, trace Abram's journey based on your chapter 11 observations. Jot down the major events that occurred next to each location.

3. Now, think about what you learned from the cross-references. What did you learn about Abraham that you didn't know from observing Genesis 11?

4. Think about Abraham's example.

   a. What is your first response to God's commands? How can you learn from Abraham's example?

   b. What do you learn about *faith* from Abraham? How can you follow his example?

   c. List below some things God says to do in His Word that you don't fully understand.

   d. Now if you are going to be like Abraham, what should your response be to these things?

   e. Take a moment alone with God. Ask, "God, do I walk in obedience? Do I walk in faith? Are there things in my life You have called me to, but I haven't started doing them?" Wait for His answer and record your thoughts below.

> Abram didn't know where he was going...but by faith he obeyed.
>
> You don't know where God will lead you today, tomorrow or 10 years from now...but you can decide now that you want to follow Him.

LESSON THREE

1. Read Genesis 11:27-12:9 using your Observation Worksheets.

    a. In this study you will focus on what you learn about Abram and the Lord. Marking these names will help you observe exactly what God tells you about Abraham and Himself in Genesis. Mark *Abram* the way you did on your bookmark. Add the *Lord* to it and mark these references with a purple triangle colored in yellow since God is Light. (If you have The New Inductive Study Bible, you might want to transfer your markings to it after you have worked through your Observation Worksheets.)

    b. While you won't always mark every reference to Abram in the study, you will find it helpful to mark them in this passage because it will train your eye to observe details about him. When you finish, list below anything you learn about the Lord and Abram that answers the 5 Ws and H: who, what, when, where, why, and how.

> The goal of Bible study is to KNOW GOD! Always look at what the scriptures teach about Him.

For example, start your list by recording Terah as Abram's father since that helps describe who Abram is. Then note the chapter and verse that give you that information.

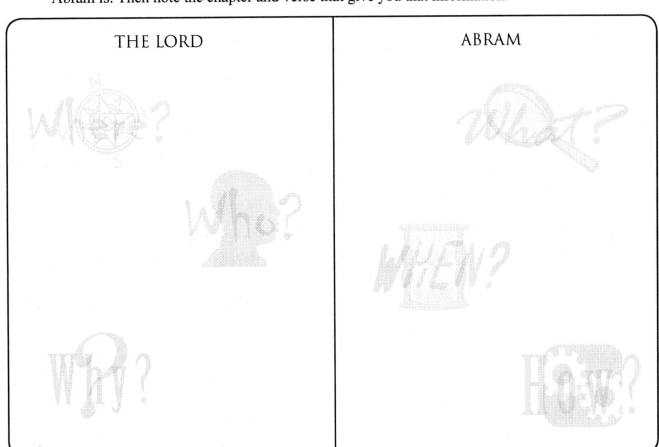

THE LORD	ABRAM

2. Read Genesis 12:1-3 again and summarize exactly what God promised Abram. List the main points of God's promise. This will help you remember exactly what God told Abram.

> Take a few minutes to reflect on the Lord. What did you notice the Lord doing and what does this tell you about Him? When you watch what God does and says, you learn much about Him. While the Bible is progressive revelation, its roots of truth are found in Genesis – the book of beginnings. Genesis shows us how God first revealed Himself to those He created for His will and pleasure (Revelation 4:11).

3. Throughout your study of Abraham, you'll learn so much about God that it's a good idea to start a "Journal on God." In fact, it's good to continue this journal throughout your study of God's Word. You'll find pages for this journal in the Appendix.

Record at least three things you learned about God from this passage in your journal and how they apply to your life.

Application is simply asking "So what?" After you've seen what the text says and understood what it means, it's time to ask yourself "so what?" What difference will the truths you've learned make in your beliefs and behavior? If they make no difference, then you should ask why. If learning about God's character and His plan and purpose for your life doesn't impact you, then you are missing the point as well as the power and blessing of Bible study.

A CLOSER LOOK AT THE LORD:

When LORD is printed in all capital letters in the New American Standard text, it is indicating the most holy name for God, YHWH. God's special or proper name, YHWH, will always be indicated as LORD in the text unless you see Lord God. In that case, Adonai is printed Lord and YHWH is printed God. You see this in Genesis 15:2.

THE MORE YOU KNOW...

Today you will read Genesis 11:27-12:9 again, identifying and marking repeated key words. Review what you learned about God and Abram.

1. Mark the following key words in this passage:

   a. *bless (blessing, blessed)* with a blue cloud ☁

   b. *land* with a double underline in green

   c. *altar* with a purple circle.

   Continue to mark these three words throughout your study and add them to your key word bookmark.

> **Key Words** – These important words, if removed, would leave the text **void** of meaning. They are often repeated.
>
> God repeated words for emphasis. Since the Bible was an **oral** book until the invention of the printing press in the 15th Century, this repetition aided in memorization.

   d. Also mark every reference to *Lot* since he will become a key figure in later chapters.

Now, did you see any references to time? Paying attention to time is very important because it answers questions like "When?" "How long?" "How old?" etc. God has a purpose when He tells you the age of someone. References to Abram's age will help you understand when various things happened in his life and how long he waited for God's promise to come to pass.

2. Read through Genesis 11:27–12:9 and mark references to time. You might mark them with a green clock like this: ⏱. This makes it easy to see.

3. Pay attention also to geographical locations since they answer the question, "Where?" Read through Genesis 11:27-12:9 and double underline in green every reference to geographical locations – places where things happened and where people went.

4. Now look at the maps located in the Appendix. Continue tracing Abram's journey through Genesis 12:9 and list below the main events (if there are any) that took place at each location.

Think of what has happened in Abram's life so far. God tells him to move, leave his home and family, all that is familiar, and go...basically, start walking. Meanwhile, he loses his father and brother, assumes responsibility for his nephew, and still has no child – not to mention he's still on a long, physically-demanding journey. In spite of these difficulties, does he get overwhelmed? Does he give up or ask God how He can expect obedience in the midst of hurting and hard times?

No! Abram obeys. Moreover, he worships! When hardship comes, he doesn't turn around and go home. Why not? What kept Abram going? Promises!

Your journey of faith may be similar! You may encounter deep valleys of sorrow and loss, and giant mountains of impossibilities and doubt. Do you have promises to cling to when the going gets tough? You do! Do you know them? You need to! If you know and believe them, you too can obey <u>and</u> worship regardless of your circumstances. God's promises are in His Word. Study and live by them!

1.   Read Genesis 12:10-20. Mark key words from your bookmark along with references to time and geographical locations. Also mark references to the *Lord*.

2. List main events from Genesis 12:10-20 below or in the margin of your Observation Worksheets.

3. Do you think Abram found good solutions to the problems in verses 10 and 12? Note the problem, Abram's solution, and what you think about it. (*Hint: Think about what God told him in 12:1-3.*)

PROBLEM IN VERSE 10:

SOLUTION:

GOOD OR BAD? WHY?

PROBLEM IN VERSE 12:

SOLUTION:

GOOD OR BAD? WHY?

4. What has Abram's experience taught you? Think through the questions below.

a. When you encounter problems, how do you solve them?

b. Have your solutions ever backfired on you?

c. What did you learn from Abram's example that you can apply to your life? How will you imitate him? How will you learn from his mistakes?

5. What did you learn about God from this passage? Record it in your "Journal on God."

6. Does this help you in any way? Don't just answer yes or no; explain your answer.

LESSON SIX

1. Today read Genesis 13 and mark key words from your bookmark, time phrases, and geographical locations. Check these locations on your map to know exactly where Abram and Lot go and what occurs in these places.

 Also, continue marking *Lot* and look carefully at references to the *land* God promised to Abram.

2. Go back to each place you marked *altar* and record its location. Note why it was built and what event happened there.

 3. Now, list what you learn from marking references to *Lot* on the "Profile of Lot" chart in the Appendix.

4. Did you notice what God tells Abram *after* Lot separates from him? Record it below.

5. Think about Genesis 12:1 and Acts 7:2-5. Do you see any possible correlation in the timing of God's promise to Abram regarding the land and Lot's departure?

6. Now think about each man's land.

a. What do you learn about the land that Lot chose and the people that lived there?

b. Where did Abram settle?

c. Where did Abram move his tent in verse 18 and what did he do there?

> Conflict and strife – it's frustrating, hurtful and even the "bigger" person can come out the loser. At first glance, Abram seems shortchanged in this conflict. However, when you look at what God tells him after he and Lot separated, do you see it differently? It seems God really can cause "all things to work together for good to those who love God, to those who are called according to His purpose." (Romans 8:28)

1.　　Read Genesis 14 and mark key words from your bookmark, references to time, geographical locations, and references to *Lot* and *Melchizedek*.

2.　Record main events from chapter 14 below or in the margin of your Observation Worksheets. You have an example below to get you started.

> v. 1-3 – Four kings vs. five kings
> v. 4-5 – Five kings served Chedorlaomer 12 years – rebelled in 13th year
> v. 5-7 – In 14th year, Chedorlaomer and the three kings with him came against them

3.　Now read Genesis 14:17-24 again. Melchizedek isn't mentioned much in the Bible, but he is a very significant character as you will see. Record everything you learn about him from this passage on the chart at the end of this lesson.

4.　Read Psalm 110:4; Hebrews 5:5-6; and 6:19–7:22. Record what you learn about Melchizedek on the chart at the end of this lesson.

5.　Did you notice how the Lord is referred to in Genesis 14:17-24? God Most High is El Elyon in Hebrew, and this is the first time God is referred to in this way. El Elyon is the name connected with the sovereignty of God and is found prominently in the book of Daniel. In your "Journal on God," note what you learn about the Lord from this.

EL ELYON
"GOD MOST HIGH"

6. Since God is the possessor of heaven and earth, what does this mean to you? How should you view the world or live your life in light of this truth?

7. Record the main event of each chapter in the appropriate place on the "Genesis 1-25 At A Glance" chart, located in the Appendix. As we continue our study of Abraham, you will add to this chart. At the end it will serve as a "table of contents" for these chapters.

8. You have just met Abram and watched him begin his walk with God. Take a few minutes to reflect on what you've seen about Abram and God. What have you learned that you can cling to or practice? Write your thoughts in the "My Journal" in the Appendix.

MELCHIZEDEK

INSIGHTS FROM GENESIS	INSIGHTS FROM PSALMS & HEBREWS
What?	 How?
 Why?	 Where?
When?	Who?

ENRICHMENT WORDS:

Ancestor – one from whom a person is descended and usually more remote than a grandparent.

El Elyon – God Most High.

Extraordinary – exceptional.

Oral – related to the mouth or speaking.

Void – containing nothing or nothing significant.

Promise Me

When you think about a **promise**, what comes to mind? What kinds of promises do people make? How often are they kept?

Sadly, society today doesn't place a lot of value on kept promises. Many "until death do us part"s are broken. Politicians rarely follow through on their promises to the public. And every day promises like "that was the last time... I promise" or "I'll never do that... I promise" or even, "I'll always love you... I promise" are broken over and over again.

If promises are unreliable, why make them? Why accept them? Is there anyone you can trust to stand by what he said? Yes! There is! The Bible says God cannot lie; He is incapable of falsehood (Titus 1:2). Don't you want to know the promises made to you by a God who cannot lie?

In this unit you will be introduced to one of the most exciting and clarifying truths in all the Word of God – **Covenant**! You will find out what God has promised and how His promises can change your life!

ONE ON ONE:

Begin this unit by asking God to show you His promises and ask Him to give you the faith to believe them. Write out your prayer below.

LESSON ONE

1. Read Genesis 15, located in the Appendix, and follow the instructions below:

    a. Examine the chapter in the light of the 5 Ws and H, and answer the following questions:

        Who, What, When, Where, Why and How – Observe the text by asking these questions as you read. This will help you read with purpose. Avoid skimming or scanning the passage as quickly as you can... you need to carefully observe what it says to accurately interpret its meaning.

        1) **Who** are the featured persons in this chapter?

        2) **What** is the progression of events?

        3) **What** is promised?

        4) To **whom** is the promise made?

        5) **When** will the promise be fulfilled?

        6) **Why** is the promise made?

    b. Mark key words and persons in distinctive ways. Be sure to include the following:

        1) references to *the land* promised to Abram and his descendants.

        2) *descendants* (Abraham's). The literal Hebrew word is "seed."

        3) references to time with a green clock ⏰ .

        4) *covenant*. You might want to color covenant red (showing that it is a bond made in blood) and then box it in yellow (since God administers them).

A CLOSER LOOK AT COVENANT:

Covenant is one key word you'll want to mark throughout your Bible. It is used approximately 298 times and is very significant because everything God does is based on covenant. The Hebrew word translated covenant is *berith*; it's a solemn binding agreement made by passing through pieces of flesh.[1]

When it's used between nations, it's a treaty, an alliance of friendship; between individuals, it's a pledge or agreement; and between God and man, it's "a covenant accompanied by signs, sacrifices, and a solemn oath that seals the relationship with promises of blessing for keeping the covenant and curses for breaking it."[2]

THE MORE YOU KNOW...

2. Now answer the following questions to help you see what is going on here.

    a. When did the Lord come to Abram? After what events?

    b. What does God say to Abram?

> Genesis 15: 1 can also be translated, "I am your shield, your very great reward!"

    c. Why do you think God reveals Himself this way to Abram? (Hint: Think about what Abram refused in Genesis 14.)

[1] James Strong, *"Hebrew and Chaldee Dictionary"* in *Strong's Exhaustive Concordance of the Bible* (Nashville, Tennessee: Holman Bible Publishers), p. 24, #1285.

[2] Elmer Smick, "Covenant," in Theological Wordbook of the Old Testament, R. Laird Harris, Gleason L. Archer, and Bruce Waltke, eds., (Chicago, Illinois: Moody Press, 1980), I, p. 128, #282a. Used by permission.

d. Is God your shield? Is He your protection, your very present help in a time of trouble? Have you taken refuge in Him?

To answer the questions above, ask yourself the following: "Who do I turn to when things go wrong? Where do I run to for help?" Write out your thoughts below.

e. What question does Abram ask God?

f. What does God tell him about his **heir**?

3. List God's promises to Abram in the margin of your Genesis 12 Observation Worksheet next to verses 1-3. Then on your Genesis 15 Observation Worksheet, list God's promise to Abram in verse 4. (It's good to keep track of God's promises to Abram so you can see how He fulfills them later in Scripture.)

LESSON TWO

What difference does a promise made thousands of years ago make in your life? Today you will begin to see how the events of Genesis 15 have a direct impact on your life.

1. Picture the events of the day described in Genesis 15. (Remember, this event occurred between a real man and God – an event that would have universal ramifications for all mankind.) Summarize in list form what happened on this day.

2. Now take a moment and sketch what happened. Draw each event in a box to show the sequence.

3. Spend the remainder of the day adding new insights you have learned from this chapter to your "Journal on God."

In your study, you want to learn all you can about Abraham and God. You need to know God and understand His ways with men. Remember, He doesn't change – He's the one you can always trust, always find refuge in. He is the unchanging source of truth you can rely on, hold on to, and live by. Truth is never **relative** to the times. Let your prayer be, "Teach me Thy ways, my God, that I might walk in them and bring You pleasure."

LESSON THREE

Genesis 15 gives us the second occurrence of *covenant* in the Word of God. The word *covenant* is used for the first time with Noah before and after the flood in Genesis 6 and 9. As you continue to study the Bible you will see that everything God does is based on covenant. Today you will look more closely at the fulfillment of the covenant in Genesis and at the covenant God made in Exodus with the children of Israel.

> **Listing** is an important observation tool. It helps you isolate information about a topic for closer examination. Writing out details helps you remember what you read. And putting information on a chart helps you easily compare information from a passage with information from related cross-references.

1. In Genesis 15:12-14, God tells Abram what will happen to his descendants (seed). List these things in the first column below. Note references to time.

WHAT IS PROPHESIED IN GENESIS 15	WHERE & HOW IT IS FULFILLED IN EXODUS

2. Read the following passages in your Bible. Watch for the word *covenant*. You might want to mark it in your Bible the same way you did on your Observation Worksheets. List how each of these prophecies about Abram's descendents are fulfilled in the second column of the chart.

   a. Exodus 2

   b. Exodus 3:20-22

   c. Exodus 11:2-3

   d. Exodus 12:33-36

   > Marking "covenant" as you read through the Word of God is an important discipline that will help you understand how the whole Bible fits together.

   e. What did you learn about God from the cross-references? You can list them below or write them in your "Journal on God."

LESSON FOUR

PRECEPT
UPON
PRECEPT®

Abraham
U-2, Lesson 4, Chapter 15

Today you will continue looking at what God says about the topic of covenant. Remember, a covenant is serious business! It is a solemn, binding oath between God and man.

1. Read Exodus 24 – an account of the Mosaic Covenant (the Law).

   In Exodus 20 God gives Moses the Ten Commandments; then He gives ordinances.

   In Exodus 23:31-33 He commands His people not to covenant with the people living in the land He promised to Abraham and his descendants or with their gods.

 In Exodus 24 the covenant of the Law is **inaugurated**. As you read this chapter, mark *covenant*. The Observation Worksheet is located at the end of this lesson.

2. List below the main things that occur in this chapter.

Good work! Although you may not understand yet why you are looking at these other covenants in Scripture, keep working. You are putting together a puzzle that once complete will show you how God included YOU in the covenant He made with Abraham. Remember, understanding God's Word is not difficult, but it does take time and effort! Keep up the good work!!

EXODUS 24

1 Then He said to Moses, "Come up to the Lord, you and Aaron, Nadab and Abihu and seventy of the elders of Israel, and you shall worship at a distance.

2 "Moses alone, however, shall come near to the Lord, but they shall not come near, nor shall the people come up with him."

3 Then Moses came and recounted to the people all the words of the Lord and all the ordinances; and all the people answered with one voice and said, "All the words which the Lord has spoken we will do!"

4 Moses wrote down all the words of the Lord. Then he arose early in the morning, and built an altar at the foot of the mountain with twelve pillars for the twelve tribes of Israel.

5 He sent young men of the sons of Israel, and they offered burnt offerings and sacrificed young bulls as peace offerings to the Lord.

6 Moses took half of the blood and put it in basins, and the other half of the blood he sprinkled on the altar.

7 Then he took the book of the covenant and read it in the hearing of the people; and they said, "All that the Lord has spoken we will do, and we will be obedient!"

8 So Moses took the blood and sprinkled it on the people, and said, "Behold the blood of the covenant, which the Lord has made with you in accordance with all these words."

9 Then Moses went up with Aaron, Nadab and Abihu, and seventy of the elders of Israel,

10 and they saw the God of Israel; and under His feet there appeared to be a pavement of sapphire, as clear as the sky itself.

11 Yet He did not stretch out His hand against the nobles of the sons of Israel; and they saw God, and they ate and drank.

12 Now the Lord said to Moses, "Come up to Me on the mountain and remain there, and I will give you the stone tablets with the law and the commandment which I have written for their instruction."

13   So Moses arose with Joshua his servant, and Moses went up to the mountain of God.

14   But to the elders he said, "Wait here for us until we return to you. And behold, Aaron and Hur are with you; whoever has a legal matter, let him approach them."

15   Then Moses went up to the mountain, and the cloud covered the mountain.

16   The glory of the Lord rested on Mount Sinai, and the cloud covered it for six days; and on the seventh day He called to Moses from the midst of the cloud.

17   And to the eyes of the sons of Israel the appearance of the glory of the Lord was like a consuming fire on the mountain top.

18   Moses entered the midst of the cloud as he went up to the mountain; and Moses was on the mountain forty days and forty nights.

Today you will look at one more covenant – the New Covenant.

1. Read Jeremiah 31:31-37 at the end of this lesson. Mark the word *covenant*. Note whether it's talking about the Old Covenant – the Law – or the New Covenant. You can distinguish them by circling references to the Old Covenant in black after you have marked it.

2. List what you learn from this text about the Old Covenant that God made with the children of Israel – the descendants of Abraham through Isaac, his son Jacob, and Jacob's twelve sons, the sons of Israel. Then list what you learn about the New Covenant in the next column.

THE OLD COVENANT	THE NEW COVENANT

3. Now look at Ezekiel 36:26-27 at the end of this lesson.

   a. Although *covenant* is not used in this passage, we see what happens once the new covenant is accepted. This is affirmed in 2 Corinthians 3:3.

> You are our letter, written in our hearts, known and read by all men; being manifested that you are a letter of Christ, cared for by us, written not with ink but with the Spirit of the living God, not on tablets of stone but on tablets of human hearts.
> – 2 Corinthians 3:2-3
>
> Paul is writing this to believers – those who are part of the New Covenant. Do you understand how he describes them in light of Ezekiel?

b. Record what will happen according to these verses.

That's a lot to take in, isn't it? God gave the Old Covenant, the Law, to the people and although they promised to obey it, they broke their promise. God kept His end of the covenant, but they did not... so what is God going to do? Does He just give up on them? No! He makes a new promise to them – one that will <u>give</u> them the ability to do what is right. Wow!! Do you have something to add to your "Journal on God" about His **grace**? Maybe you should right now.

JEREMIAH 31:31-37

31 "Behold, days are coming," declares the LORD, "when I will make a new covenant with the house of Israel and with the house of Judah,

32 not like the covenant which I made with their fathers in the day I took them by the hand to bring them out of the land of Egypt, My covenant which they broke, although I was a husband to them," declares the LORD.

33 "But this is the covenant which I will make with the house of Israel after those days," declares the LORD, "I will put My law within them and on their heart I will write it; and I will be their God, and they shall be My people.

34 "They will not teach again, each man his neighbor and each man his brother, saying, 'Know the LORD,' for they will all know Me, from the least of them to the greatest of them," declares the LORD, "for I will forgive their iniquity, and their sin I will remember no more."

35   Thus says the LORD,

Who gives the sun for light by day

And the fixed order of the moon and the stars for light by night,

Who stirs up the sea so that its waves roar;

The LORD of hosts is His name:

36   "If this fixed order departs

From before Me," declares the LORD,

"Then the offspring of Israel also will cease

From being a nation before Me forever."

37   Thus says the LORD,

"If the heavens above can be measured

And the foundations of the earth searched out below,

Then I will also cast off all the offspring of Israel

For all that they have done," declares the LORD.

EZEKIEL 36:26-27

26   "Moreover, I will give you a new heart and put a new spirit within you; and I will remove the heart of stone from your flesh and give you a heart of flesh.

27   "I will put My Spirit within you and cause you to walk in My statutes, and you will be careful to observe My ordinances.

LESSON SIX

Today you will see how *you* fit into what you've been learning about and how these three covenants, the Abrahamic, Old, and New, fit together. Are you ready? This is exciting!!!

1. Read Galatians 3, which is printed out at the end of this lesson. Mark the following along with any pronouns (some marking suggestions are provided):

   a.   *Abraham*

   b.   *covenant*

   c. *promise*

   d. *Law* with stone tablets

   e. *faith* with a purple book, shaded green

   f. *descendants* in verse 29 (literally *seed*)

   g. *Spirit* with a purple cloud, shaded yellow

   h. *Jesus Christ* with a purple cross, shaded yellow.

   > In this chapter Paul asks several questions similar to the one, "If all your friends jumped off a bridge, would you?" The obvious answer is "No!" Paul is helping the reader understand his point by asking questions with obvious answers. Look for these rhetorical questions and determine what Paul is trying to get his audience to understand.

2. List what you learned about the *Law*, the Old Covenant. The first few are listed for you.

   v. 2, 5   *Did not receive the Spirit by works of the Law*
   v. 10   *Works of the Law are under a curse*
            Cursed is everyone who does not abide by all that is written in the Law

Now, answer the following questions:

   a. When did the Law come (after what covenant)?

   b. Why was the Law given?

   c. What does "kept in **custody**" mean?

3. List what you learned from Galatians about the promises God gave Abraham.

   a. Who is blessed *with* Abraham?

4. Before you list your observations on the New Covenant, review Ezekiel 36:27. What did God promise to give in the New Covenant?

a. List your observations on *faith*.

> Do you know what a **Gentile** is? If you are not Jewish, descended from Abraham, <u>you</u> are!

b. How do you receive the promise of the Spirit? In other words, how do you participate in the New Covenant?

c. According to verse 26, what do you have to believe?

d. Finally, how is God's promise to Abraham fulfilled in the New Covenant? How are "all the nations" blessed in him?

THE THREE COVENANTS PROJECT

For this project you will need:

a posterboard and *creativity!*

Divide a posterboard into three sections. Label the first section, "Abrahamic Covenant"; the second section, "The Law"; and the third section, "The New Covenant." Under each title, answer as many of the following questions as you can from what you have learned about each covenant.

1. When? (When was it made? How long will it last?)

2. Who? (Who made it? Who was it made with?)

3. What? (What was promised? What was its purpose?)

4. What was the outcome? (What was Abram's response? What was Israel's response? What should be the response of those participating in the New Covenant?)

Now, next to each answer, find a way to creatively represent each point. You can use any materials you want to complete this part of the project, including drawings or pictures from magazines, newspapers, etc. *(For example: You can represent the promise of a descendent to Abram by gluing a seed next to this point.)*

GALATIANS 3

1   You foolish Galatians, who has bewitched you, before whose eyes Jesus Christ was publicly portrayed as crucified?

2   This is the only thing I want to find out from you: did you receive the Spirit by the works of the Law, or by hearing with faith?

3   Are you so foolish? Having begun by the Spirit, are you now being perfected by the flesh?

4   Did you suffer so many things in vain—if indeed it was in vain?

5   So then, does He who provides you with the Spirit and works miracles among you, do it by the works of the Law, or by hearing with faith?

6   Even so Abraham believed God, and it was reckoned to him as righteousness.

7   Therefore, be sure that it is those who are of faith who are sons of Abraham.

8   The Scripture, foreseeing that God would justify the Gentiles by faith, preached the gospel beforehand to Abraham, saying, "All the nations will be blessed in you."

9   So then those who are of faith are blessed with Abraham, the believer.

10   For as many as are of the works of the Law are under a curse; for it is written, "Cursed is everyone who does not abide by all things written in the book of the law, to perform them."

11   Now that no one is justified by the Law before God is evident; for, "The righteous man shall live by faith. "

12   However, the Law is not of faith; on the contrary, "He who practices them shall live by them."

13   Christ redeemed us from the curse of the Law, having become a curse for us—for it is written, "Cursed is everyone who hangs on a tree"—

14   in order that in Christ Jesus the blessing of Abraham might come to the Gentiles, so that we might receive the promise of the Spirit through faith.

15   Brethren, I speak in terms of human relations: even though it is only a man's covenant, yet when it has been ratified, no one sets it aside or adds conditions to it.

16   Now the promises were spoken to Abraham and to his seed. He does not say, "And to seeds," as referring to many, but rather to one, "And to your seed," that is, Christ.

17   What I am saying is this: the Law, which came four hundred and thirty years later, does not invalidate a covenant previously ratified by God, so as to nullify the promise.

18   For if the inheritance is based on law, it is no longer based on a promise; but God has granted it to Abraham by means of a promise.

19   Why the Law then? It was added because of transgressions, having been ordained through angels by the agency of a mediator, until the seed would come to whom the promise had been made.

20   Now a mediator is not for one party only; whereas God is only one.

21   Is the Law then contrary to the promises of God? May it never be! For if a law had been given which was able to impart life, then righteousness would indeed have been based on law.

22   But the Scripture has shut up everyone under sin, so that the promise by faith in Jesus Christ might be given to those who believe.

23   But before faith came, we were kept in custody under the law, being shut up to the faith which was later to be revealed.

24   Therefore the Law has become our tutor to lead us to Christ, so that we may be justified by faith.

25   But now that faith has come, we are no longer under a tutor.

26   For you are all sons of God through faith in Christ Jesus.

27   For all of you who were baptized into Christ have clothed yourselves with Christ.

28   There is neither Jew nor Greek, there is neither slave nor free man, there is neither male nor female; for you are all one in Christ Jesus.

29   And if you belong to Christ, then you are Abraham's descendants, heirs according to promise.

LESSON SEVEN

PRECEPT
UPON
PRECEPT®

Abraham
U-2, Lesson 7, Chapter 15

Today you're going to take a break from your studies on the three covenants and look more closely at Abram's response to God's promises.

1. Genesis 15:6 is a very significant verse. It is quoted in three New Testament books. Look up each quotation, consider its context, and write down what you learn. What does it tell you about Abraham?

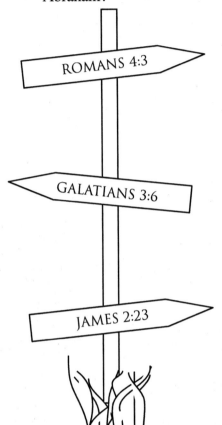

a. Read verses 1-8 for the full context.

b. Read verses 1-9 for the full context.

c. James is showing his letter's recipients that works accompany genuine faith. Real faith is seen in what it produces. Watch the word "fulfilled" in this verse. Note *what* was fulfilled and *how*. What did Abraham do that proved his faith was real?

2. Now based on the passages you just read, how would you answer the following questions?

a. How is a person saved?

b. What is the example?

c. Why does Paul refer to Abraham in Galatians 3?

d. What does he want his readers to understand?

e. Examine your life in light of James' teaching. What evidence supports *your* claim to be a genuine Christian?

3. Finally, draw a timeline below and place the Abrahamic, Mosaic, and New Covenants in chronological order. Then under each covenant, write what it provided or promised.

4.   Don't forget to add new insights to your "Journal on God."

5.   Add the main event(s) in chapter 15 to your "Genesis 1-25 At A Glance" chart.

Were you diligent in this lesson? It was a lot of work, but understanding God's amazing promises is worth the time!! Do you realize how awesome it is that God included you in His promise to Abraham? As far back as Abraham, and further, He knew He would send Jesus to die for you so that you could enter into the New Covenant. Take a few moments to stop and thank God for His grace, wisdom, and plan.

ENRICHMENT WORDS:

Covenant – a solemn binding agreement made by passing through pieces of flesh.

Custody – to protect by guarding; to keep.

Gentile – a non Jew.

Grace – good will, loving-kindness, favor.

Heir – one who receives or is entitled to receive an endowment or quality from a parent or predecessor.

Inaugurate – to bring about the beginning of.

Promise – declaration that one will do or refrain from doing something specified.

Relative – a thing connected with or dependent on another thing.

Impossibilities

Is anything too difficult for the Lord? The answer ingrained in your head is probably no. But, does your life – your choices and actions – reflect a genuine faith that God is able to accomplish all that He has promised?

If you believe nothing is too difficult for God, what will you base your decisions on? How will you respond to authority? Will other people see a difference in your attitude, especially in the midst of difficult circumstances?

In this unit you're going to see God ask Abraham this question. And you will see how Abraham fails and succeeds. Study diligently and you will learn how to succeed where Abraham failed and imitate him when he was faithful!

ONE ON ONE: PRAYER

Begin Unit Three by writing a prayer. Tell God what bothers you, what **insurmountable** things you face, and what you think should be different if you believe He is what He says He is... or what you wish were different and why. Pour out your heart; be honest. At the end of the unit, you can go back to your prayer and see how God answers and what He has taught you through His Word.

LESSON ONE

1. Read Genesis 12:1-3 and Genesis 15:1-6, and answer the following questions:

   a. What does God promise Abram in Genesis 12:3?

   b. What has to happen for this promise to be fulfilled?

   c. According to Genesis 11:30, what was Sarai's status as a mother?

   d. According to Genesis 15:1-4, what does Abram assume about the heir of his household?

   e. How does God respond to Abram's concern? How does He say it will happen?

2. Now read Genesis 16:1-3. What is Sarai's solution to her barrenness?

3. Have you ever tried to help God out – speed up His answers to your prayers? Ever tried to **manipulate** a situation to get something you want? If so, this unit holds many lessons for life for you and will deepen your understanding of God and Abram.

   Take a few minutes to write below circumstances you have been trying to manipulate instead of waiting on God.

4. Observe Genesis 16. Mark key words as you have done previously, and give careful attention to references to time/age; mark them with a clock. Also, mark the following, but don't add them to your bookmark:

      a.   *Hagar* with a purple underline

      b.   *Ishmael* with a brown box

  c.   *the angel of the Lord* shaded yellow

LESSON TWO

PRECEPT
UPON
PRECEPT®

Abraham
U-3, Lesson 2, Chapter 16

ADONAI
"LORD"

In Genesis 15:2, Abram calls God "**Adonai,**" which is translated "Lord." This is the first time "Adonai" is used. (Remember, YHWH is translated "GOD" when it appears with Adonai.) In Genesis 16:13, Hagar calls the Lord, "**El Roi**" – *the* God *who* sees.

EL ROI
"THE GOD
WHO SEES"

1. How do these two names of God help you understand what God is like? Record your insights. Consider the context these names are introduced in as you answer.

2. Fill in the information about Abram's first son and his mother on the "Abraham's Family Tree" chart in the Appendix. Then, summarize what the angel of the Lord said about him.

3. Think about Genesis 16 in light of the previous chapters you've studied, then record what you think about:

   a. Abram's actions in respect to Sarai's suggestion

   b. Sarai's reaction to Abram after Hagar conceives

   c. the Angel of the Lord's treatment of Hagar (What does this tell you about God?)

In a desperate moment, Hagar recognizes that God sees her in the midst of her difficulty. She is told that she must go back to the situation she's running from and submit to authority.

4. Have you ever felt like Hagar? Do you know what it's like to be used and rejected? Based on what you learned in this chapter, what do you think God wants you to do? Write out your thoughts.

5. Why doesn't God doesn't always deliver us from difficult circumstances? Read the verse in the pull-out box and write out your answer below.

> "Consider it all joy, my brethren, when you encounter various trials, knowing that the testing of your faith produces endurance. And let endurance have its perfect result, so that you may be perfect and complete, lacking in nothing."
>
> – James 1:2-4

The angel of the Lord tells Hagar to name her son Ishmael, meaning "God hears." She names the place where God saw her affliction and provided a stream, Beer-lahai-roi, which means "the well of the living one who sees me."

6. What comfort do these names give Hagar? What comfort can they give you in the midst of your circumstances?

Life can be hard... really hard. The hurts people cause, even those who are supposed to love and protect us, can be too numerous to count. Where is God in the midst of these hurts? Is He blind to what is going on? Does He not care?

The story of Hagar shows that God is there, He sees everything, and He cares. God has a plan. If you obey Him and follow His leading, even when it's hard, He will "cause all things to work together for good to those who love God, to those who are called according to His purpose" (Romans 8:28).

LESSON THREE

1. Observe Genesis 17. Mark the following words:

   a. *covenant*

   b. *descendants*

   c. *circumcision* with a red symbol like this ⌣ .

2. Genesis 17:1 contains the first mention of God as **El Shaddai**, which is translated "God Almighty."

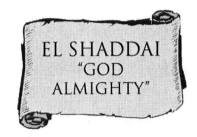

EL SHADDAI "GOD ALMIGHTY"

   a. Note the context in which God reveals Himself this way. What are the circumstances surrounding the revelation of this name?

   b. Look at the Hebrew definition for "El Shaddai" in the insight box. Look back at the context in which it is used and explain how the definition helps you understand the passage better.

1. Before you go any further in your observations of Genesis 17, answer the following questions to establish the context of this chapter:

   a. What has God done for Abram so far?

   b. What has God promised He would do?

   c. Have all of those promises been fulfilled? Explain.

   d. Up to this point, are there any conditions in God's covenant with Abram?

   e. What did God require from Abram prior to chapter 17?

2. Read Genesis 17:1-8 and mark every occurrence of *nations*. God has much to say regarding the nations; it's a word you'll want to mark consistently in any book of Scripture you are studying.

   a. Compare what you learn about the *nations* with Genesis 12:2 and 3. What do you see?

b.　List the promises God gives Abram in this chapter.

3.　List everything you learn about *circumcision* from Genesis 17.

4.　Can you see any relationship between the act of circumcision and the promise to Abraham and his seed? (At last we get to call Abram, Abraham!)

LESSON FIVE

PRECEPT
UPON
PRECEPT®

Abraham
U-3, Lesson 5, Chapter 17

1. What do you learn about Isaac and Ishmael from Genesis 17? List your insights on the chart below. Note what Abraham requests for Ishmael and God's response.

ISAAC	ISHMAEL

2. What is the time lapse between:

    a. Genesis 16 and Genesis 17?

    b. Genesis 12 and Genesis 17?

    c. God's promise of a child through Sarah and his arrival (Genesis 17:21)?

3. Although you haven't looked at the fulfillment of God's promise of a son to Abraham yet, add *Isaac* to "Abraham's Family Tree," located in the Appendix.

> How long are you willing to wait for God to fulfill His promises? Regardless of how much time passes, will you trust that He'll be faithful to His Word?

1. Carefully observe Genesis 18:1-19 and mark all key words from your bookmark. When you come to the question, *"Is anything too difficult for the Lord?"* mark it in a significant way on your Observation Worksheet and in your Bible.

2. Now, look at the setting of the question, *"Is anything too difficult for the Lord?"* Remember, these are people just like you; they are not "super-saints" who live *above it all*. Rather, they are followers of God who are living *through it all*; and through it all is not always easy!

   a. Stop and recheck the time phrases in Genesis 17. How old are Sarah and Abraham when God asks Abraham this question?

   b. Although you have already calculated this, how old is God's promise regarding the child who will inherit the promise that includes the land? How long have Abraham and Sarah been waiting on God?

   c. Why do you think Sarah laughed?

3. What do you learn about Abraham from the following passage? Look at it carefully – don't miss a thing! It's too good to miss! List your insights.

ROMANS 4:18-21

1. Spend today digging a little deeper into Genesis 18:1-19.

   a. Why did Sarah deny that she laughed?

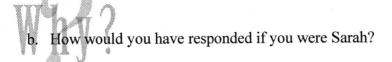

   b. How would you have responded if you were Sarah?

   c. Who is speaking to Abraham in Genesis 18:13-14?

      1) How do you know?

      2) How does he relate to the three men who stopped at Abraham and Sarah's tent?

   d. What do you learn about Abraham in Genesis 18:16-19?

   e. From reading Genesis 18:1-19, what do you learn about God?

2. Suppose God He asked you, "Is anything too difficult for the Lord?" Knowing your circumstances, how would you answer Him and why?

3. Add the main events of chapters 16-18 to your "Genesis 1-25 At A Glance" chart.

4. Record your insights about God in your "Journal on God."

5. As you bring this unit's study to a close, what is your prayer – the cry of your heart? Why don't you write it in a way that's meaningful to you? Maybe a poem, prayer, sketch, or song... who knows what God will do with it! Is anything too difficult for the Lord?

ENRICHMENT WORDS:

Adonai – Lord or Master

El Shaddai – God Almighty or God All Sufficient

El Roi – the God Who sees

Insurmountable – incapable of being prevailed over

Manipulate – to manage or utilize skillfully; to control or play upon by artful, unfair, or insidious means especially to one's own advantage

When Judgment Comes

Tolerance. What does it *really* mean? If you disagree with someone's world view, lifestyle, or choices, then you are often labeled "intolerant" sometimes even **phobic** or **bigoted**. But matters most? God's opinion or man's?

What does God say about **controversial** moral issues like immorality, homosexuality, and judgment? In this unit you'll find out from the scriptures yourself.

You already know what the world says. You are bombarded with opinions, "scientific" evidence, and pressure everyday to believe someone else's point of view. But once you see for yourself what God says, you'll have to decided if you agree with Him. If you are going to view the world biblically and if you have chosen to be a follower of Christ, then you need to know the truth, God's truth! Remember only one truth promises to set you free – free to live the abundant life God has called you to, free to love others as Christ did. What will you choose?

PRAYER ONE ON ONE:

The Word of God is relevant. And requires you to look at the world around you *through* the lens of Scripture versus the lens of the world. Over the next few days God will communicate truth that demands action. As you gear up for what God says in this unit, take time to commit your study to Him in prayer. Ask Him to renew your mind with His truth!

LESSON ONE

1. Read Genesis 18 to understand the context for this week's study.

2. Now, observe Genesis 18:16-19:38, marking key words from your bookmark including *Lot*.

> **Context** is the setting, the environment where something occurs. Read this chapter to get the big picture before you begin to dig deeper and look at the details. This will help you interpret the details accurately.

    a. Give careful attention to the *three men* (Genesis 18:1, 2, 16) who visit Abraham and Sarah. Notice how the text describes them – the specific word(s) used to indicate what they are. Mark them with an orange 3.

    b. If you haven't already marked geographical references, double underline every location to know exactly where everything occurs. Consult the maps in the Appendix.

    c. Mark references to *destroy* and its synonyms with red, fiery flames. Observe what is destroyed, how and why.

> A synonym is a word that means the same thing as another.

1. In the previous lesson you marked key words and characters in Genesis 18:16–19:38. The people mentioned in these verses are extremely important. Fill in the chart below and on the following page by listing in the appropriate box what the text says about each character.

THREE MEN	GOD	LOT

ABRAHAM	LOT'S WIFE	LOT'S DAUGHTERS	MEN OF SODOM

To say this is a disturbing story is an understatement. Although you may not understand everything, it's clear what God thought about the wickedness of Sodom and Gommorah's people. Don't be overwhelmed by these chapters! The remainder of this unit will help you understand them and why they are important to you! God recorded these events for a reason... they were written for your instruction (Romans 15:4).

LESSON THREE

When the Word of God gives a lot attention to a subject, person, or place, then you need to discover why and what you can learn. *Sodom* is mentioned 48 times in 14 books of the Bible. Your task today is to get an overview of Sodom.

1. Look up the following passages and record what you learn on the chart "What the Bible Says about Sodom" at the end of this lesson. As you observe:

    a.   Mark references to *Sodom* with a black S.

    b. Check each reference's context and ask the 5 Ws and H: who (to whom is God referring? comparing? likening?) what, when, where, why and how.

    c. Ask about Sodom's **pertinence** to God's people in Old Testament days and to you today. Record these insights in the column "Lessons to be Learned."

GENESIS 10:19
(*Check your map*)

GENESIS 13:10-13

GENESIS 14:2,8,10-12,17,21-22

GENESIS 18-19

DEUTERONOMY 29:23

DEUTERONOMY 32:32

ISAIAH 3:9

JEREMIAH 23:14

JEREMIAH 50:40

LAMENTATIONS 4:6

EZEKIEL 16:46-55

ZEPHANIAH 2:9

MATTHEW 11:23-24

JUDE 1:7

WHAT THE BIBLE SAYS ABOUT SODOM

VERSE	WHAT THE TEXT SAYS ABOUT SODOM	LESSONS TO BE LEARNED

Did you realize that the Word of God has so much to say about Sodom? Many today say that Sodom was only discussed in the Old Testament; however, you have seen that even Jesus discussed Sodom in Matthew! Think about how relevant this is, and there is more to come! We still have a lot to learn about Lot. You've accomplished a lot of work in the past few lessons. Great job!

1. From all you observed in Genesis 18-19, what sin of Sodom was "exceedingly grave" (Genesis 18:20)? It's important that you see this for yourself so that if you ever discuss the issue with others, you'll know. Write it below and supporting your answer with Scripture.

2. What do you learn about the Lord from this account in Genesis 18:16-19:29?

   a. Read through the text again and watch for every mention of the *Lord*, then record what you learn about God from this text.

b. Read Genesis 18:20-21 and Genesis 11:6-9 and note every reference to the *Lord*. Record in the appropriate column what you learn about Him.

GENESIS 18:20-21	GENESIS 11:6-9

c. How involved does God get in the affairs of men? In each of these incidents, why does God do what He does?

3. How involved do you think God is in your life? How does your answer affect the choices you make and how you respond to circumstances?

LESSON FIVE

Today you are going to look at God's Word to understand what He says about homosexuality. You need to know what God says. Many people today make claims about God's perspective on this issue that are dead wrong. You need to know the truth so you will not be deceived!

1. Look up the following passages and note what you learn from them and how they parallel with Genesis 18:16-19:29. Don't forget to check the context of the verses.

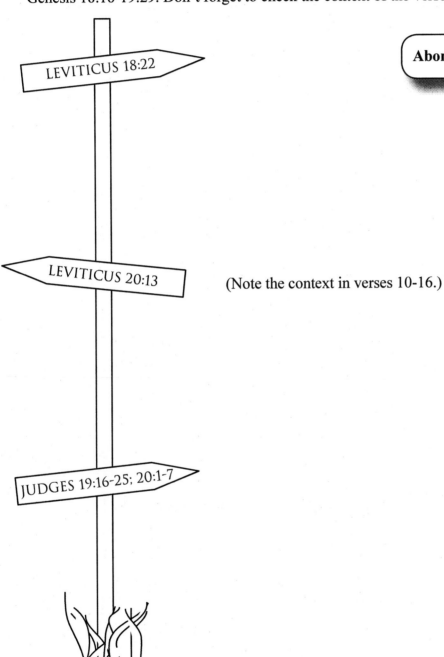

LEVITICUS 18:22

Abomination - *a disgusting thing.*

LEVITICUS 20:13

(Note the context in verses 10-16.)

JUDGES 19:16-25; 20:1-7

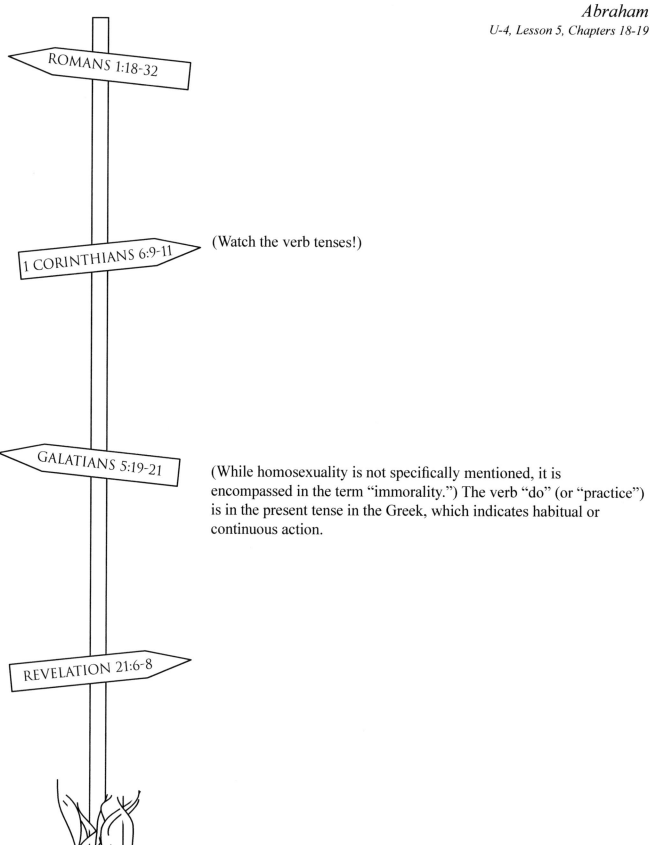

ROMANS 1:18-32

1 CORINTHIANS 6:9-11

(Watch the verb tenses!)

GALATIANS 5:19-21

(While homosexuality is not specifically mentioned, it is encompassed in the term "immorality.") The verb "do" (or "practice") is in the present tense in the Greek, which indicates habitual or continuous action.

REVELATION 21:6-8

Today you are going to discuss what you learned from Lesson Five about God's view of homosexuality.

1. Considering all you have observed:

   a. What does God say about homosexuality (the term includes lesbianism)? What does He think about this behavior?

   b. What do you think about homosexuality? Why?

   c. Do you think a person can be a practicing homosexual and genuine child of God? Give reasons for your answer.

   d. Do you think people are "born this way" and can't help it? Explain why.

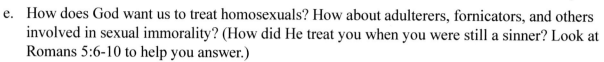

e. How does God want us to treat homosexuals? How about adulterers, fornicators, and others involved in sexual immorality? (How did He treat you when you were still a sinner? Look at Romans 5:6-10 to help you answer.)

f. What is the cure for these sins? Is there any hope? Any help? (Look carefully at 1 Corinthians 6:11.)

> Do you see a stark difference between what the world says about homosexuality and what God says? Who are you going to agree with? It's important to remember that all sin is equally worthy of judgment in God's eyes. The person guilty of lying is as worthy of death as the homosexual or immoral person. And every person, regardless of their sin, can be forgiven and redeemed through Christ's sacrifice. If you are going to be an **ambassador** for Christ you need to see sin as He sees sin and love the way He loves. "Be no longer conformed to this world, but be transformed by the renewing of your mind, so that you may prove what the will of God is, that which is good and acceptable and perfect" (Romans 12:2).

LESSON SEVEN

1. Today you will learn all you can about Lot. Look up the following verses and record what you learn about him on the "Profile of Lot" chart in the Appendix.

   a. Genesis 11:27-31; 12:4-5; 13:1-14; 14:12-16

   b. 2 Peter 2:7-8

2. Now with the information you have gleaned from Genesis, add Lot and his offspring to "Abraham's Family Tree." His descendants are important throughout the Old Testament.

3. What can you apply from Lot's life? Consider the following:

   a. How would you describe the choices Lot made?

   b. Can you relate to Lot in any way?

   c. How does Peter describe him?

   d. Does Peter's description give you hope? Explain.

   e. What can you apply from his example? How can you learn from his mistakes?

4. Add the main events of chapters 18-19 to your "Genesis 1-25 At A Glance" chart.

5. Don't forget to record new insights to your "Journal on God."

6. Memorize Genesis 18:19 and determine to follow Abraham's example.

EZEKIEL 9 PROJECT

For this project, you will need:

a Bible

Read Ezekiel 9 and write a one-page summary and response to what is happening and why.

Address the following questions in your summary and response:

1. Who receives the mark on their foreheads?

2. Where do the executioners begin their destruction?

3. Rather than mourning abominations in today's society, how do many believers respond?

4. What do you think would happen today if this same scenario took place in your church, school or community?

5. How do you respond to abominations commited in your church, school or community?

ENRICHMENT WORDS:

Abomination – extreme disgust and hatred; loathing.

Ambassador – an authorized representative or messenger.

Bigot – a person obstinately or intolerantly devoted to his or her own opinions and prejudices; especially one who regards or treats the members of a group (e.g. a racial or ethnic group) with hatred and intolerance.

Controversy – a discussion marked especially by the expression of opposing views.

Pertinence – having a clear decisive relevance to the matter at hand.

Phobic – characterized by an exaggerated, usually inexplicable and illogical fear of a particular object, class of objects, or situation.

Tolerance – a: sympathy or indulgence for beliefs or practices differing from or conflicting with one's own b: the act of allowing something.

Worth the Wait

Finally... a baby for Abraham and Sarah! A promise God gave nearly 25 years earlier is about to come to pass. They waited a long time, but God was faithful to His promise.

How long are you willing to wait for God's promises without grumbling, complaining, or losing faith? What if it takes 5, 10, 25, 50, or even a lifetime for you to realize His promises?

Think about how Isaac's long-awaited arrival can help you learn to trust and wait...

> For when God made the promise to Abraham, since He could swear by no one greater, He swore by Himself, saying, "I will surely bless you, and I will surely multiply you."
>
> And thus having patiently waited, he obtained the promise."
>
> - Hebrews 6:13-15

PRAYER ONE ON ONE:

Remember to pray before you begin your work on this unit. Write your prayer out below. Be specific, then look back when you are finished with this unit and see how God answered your prayer.

This is such a good unit – so enlightening, encouraging and liberating! Begin it with prayer.

1. Observe Genesis 20 and mark key words on your bookmark. Add the following words:

   a.   *dream* with a blue cloud .

   b.   *prayer* – mark it purple and shade it pink with a symbol like cupped hands . (Mark it the same way throughout your Bible.)

   c.   *sin*, along with synonyms *iniquity* and *transgression*. Shade them brown. (Mark them the same way throughout your Bible.)

2. Briefly summarize the main events in this chapter.

   3.   Record your summary statement of Genesis 20 on your "Genesis 1-25 At A Glance" chart.

4. Answer the following questions:

   a.   What did God promise Abraham and Sarah in Genesis 15:4 and 18:9-14? (You have already studied these, but look at them once more; they will help you understand Genesis 20.)

   b.   As you think about this promise, why did God keep Abimelech from touching Sarah? (When he took her as his wife, he had the right to sleep with her.)

c. What would have been questioned when Sarah gave birth the following year?

d. What does this tell you about God?

5. Now, take some time to think about how this truth about God can be applied to your life.

a. Has God made promises to believers that haven't come to pass? If you think of any, write them down.

b. Do you ever sin or make poor choices? (Silly question, but it's good to recognize.)

c. Based on what you learned about God from Genesis 20, can sin or poor choices hinder God from fulfilling His promises?

Isn't it awesome that God is faithful to His promises even when we mess up? You are going to sin. You are going to make poor choices. But these things will never cause God to go back on His promises. He has promised to never leave you or forsake you. He has promised eternal life to those who come to Him through His Son, Jesus Christ. He has promised to one day end suffering, trials, and pain. Some of these things haven't happened yet, but you can trust that what He has promised, He will do, and you can't do anything to stop it. Praise the Lord!

1. Observe Genesis 21:1-21, marking key words from your bookmark, noting locations, etc., as you have done before.

  a. Watch for references to time in this chapter.

  b. Also don't forget to mark references to *circumcision* – remember what you learned in Genesis 17!

This loaded chapter should be a delight to observe if you, like Abraham, have wondered when Sarah would finally have a child!

  2. Find the locations mentioned in this chapter on the maps in the Appendix.

3. How old was Sarah when she gave birth to Isaac? (Genesis 21 doesn't say, but you can figure it out from Genesis 17:17).

4. Have you wondered how Sarah could conceive a child at such an age? Two passages answer this question and provide wonderful insights to those who want to be friends of God.

HEBREWS 11:11-12

  a. Record what you learn from this passage.

 b. When you studied Abraham's **salvation** experience, you cross-referenced Romans 4:1-8. Return to Romans 4 to get more insight into Abraham's faith.

  1) Read Romans 4:13-25, which is printed at the end of the lesson. Don't mark anything yet – just take in this rich chapter.

> To be sure you accurately handle God's Word, you need to study all the places in the Bible where a subject is taught. A **cross-reference** is a reference to another Scripture that supports, illumines, or amplifies the Scripture you are studying. Comparing Scripture with Scripture will help you interpret the text without the use of commentaries.

2) Now go back and mark the following key words:

    a.   *Law* with stone tablets

    b.   *faith* (*believe*) with a purple book, shaded green

    c.   *grace* with a yellow box, shaded blue

    d.   *promise* with a large **P**

    e.   *credited* with an orange box.

3) Also mark:

    a.   *Abraham*

    b.   *Sarah*

    c.   *God* with a purple △, shaded yellow

    d.   *Jesus Christ* with a purple cross shaded yellow.

That's enough for today. In the next lesson, you will look at this passage more in-depth. Good job!

ROMANS 4:13-25

13 For the promise to Abraham or to his descendants that he would be heir of the world was not through the Law, but through the righteousness of faith.

14 For if those who are of the Law are heirs, faith is made void and the promise is nullified;

15 for the Law brings about wrath, but where there is no law, neither is there violation.

16 For this reason *it is* by faith, in order that *it may be* in accordance with grace, so that the promise will be guaranteed to all the descendants, not only to those who are of the Law, but also to those who are of the faith of Abraham, who is the father of us all,

17 (as it is written, "A FATHER OF MANY NATIONS HAVE I MADE YOU") in the presence of Him whom he believed, *even* God, who gives life to the dead and calls into being that which does not exist.

18 In hope against hope he believed, so that he might become a father of many nations according to that which had been spoken, "SO SHALL YOUR DESCENDANTS BE."

19 Without becoming weak in faith he contemplated his own body, now as good as dead since he was about a hundred years old, and the deadness of Sarah's womb;

20 yet, with respect to the promise of God, he did not waver in unbelief, but grew strong in faith, giving glory to God,

21 and being fully assured that what God had promised, He was able also to perform.

22 Therefore IT WAS ALSO CREDITED TO HIM AS RIGHTEOUSNESS.

23 Now not for his sake only was it written that it was credited to him,

24 but for our sake also, to whom it will be credited, as those who believe in Him who raised Jesus our Lord from the dead,

25 *He* who was delivered over because of our transgressions, and was raised because of our justification.

1. Now list what you observed from Hebrews 11:11-12 and Romans 4:13-25 about:

ABRAHAM	SARAH	GOD	JESUS CHRIST

2. Finally, list at least five things you have just learned and how they can help you and others who need to understand these principles of faith.

> Awesome, isn't it! Meditate on these things. Don't let these incredible truths about faith, righteousness, and God slip through your fingers by simply recording them and not thinking about their significance to you and to the whole teaching of salvation. Admire and imitate Abraham's faith.

1. Today, look again at Genesis 21:1-21. List what happened when Abraham celebrated the weaning of his son Isaac with a feast. Record who did what to whom and why.

2. Before you go further in your study of this significant event, review what God recorded about Hagar and her son Ishmael. Look up the following passages and record what you learn from them about Hagar and Ishmael: Genesis 16:1-16; 17:18-26. Note Ishmael's age in Genesis 17 because it helps put the events of Genesis 21 in perspective.

HAGAR	ISHMAEL

3. Read Galatians 4:21-31 below, marking key words as you did when you studied Galatians several weeks ago (*covenant, promise, Spirit, Law, faith*) along with the following: *Isaac, Hagar* and synonyms used for Hagar.

GALATIANS 4:21-31

21   Tell me, you who want to be under law, do you not listen to the law?

22   For it is written that Abraham had two sons, one by the bondwoman and one by the free woman.

23   But the son by the bondwoman was born according to the flesh, and the son by the free woman through the promise.

24   This is allegorically speaking, for these *women* are two covenants: one *proceeding* from Mount Sinai bearing children who are to be slaves; she is Hagar.

25   Now this Hagar is Mount Sinai in Arabia and corresponds to the present Jerusalem, for she is in slavery with her children.

26   But the Jerusalem above is free; she is our mother.

27   For it is written,

"REJOICE, BARREN WOMAN WHO DOES NOT BEAR;

BREAK FORTH AND SHOUT, YOU WHO ARE NOT IN LABOR;

FOR MORE NUMEROUS ARE THE CHILDREN OF THE DESOLATE

THAN OF THE ONE WHO HAS A HUSBAND."

28   And you brethren, like Isaac, are children of promise.

29   But as at that time he who was born according to the flesh persecuted him *who was born* according to the Spirit, so it is now also.

30   But what does the Scripture say?

"CAST OUT THE BONDWOMAN AND HER SON,

FOR THE SON OF THE BONDWOMAN SHALL NOT BE AN HEIR WITH THE SON OF THE FREE

WOMAN."

31   So then, brethren, we are not children of a bondwoman, but of the free woman.

> This is enough for now. You'll finish your study of this passage tomorrow. This is an awesome passage so don't just complete your assignment and walk away from this lesson. Think about what you have read!

1. Look at the Galatians 4 passage you marked in the last lesson. According to Galatians 4:21-31:

    a. What two covenants are contrasted in this passage?

    b. How are these covenants symbolized, allegorized? It might help to draw a diagram or sketch of what this passage is teaching.

> An allegory is a story with an underlying meaning that differs from the surface facts of the story itself; in other words, it describes one thing by using the image of another. It is used to teach one or more truths, which may or may not be related.

    c. How does this compare with Genesis 21:1-14? Give as detailed an answer as possible but only using the facts – not imagination which can often get you into theological hot water!

2. For the sake of clarity, write who the following represent in Galatians 4:

    a. The bondwoman and her children

    b. The free woman and her children

c. Now, can you see how all this fits with the message of Romans 4 and how it pertains to you? What does God want you to understand?

3. How can you apply all you've learned?

   a. Is there a "bondwoman" in your life? In other words, are you in bondage to a list of ritual do's and don'ts?

   b. How did Abraham, the friend of God, walk? On what basis did he relate to God? (Genesis 15:6)

   c. How can you live as a friend of God?

LESSON SIX

 1. In your final day of study for this unit, you are going to return to Genesis 21 and observe the rest of the chapter. Look at Genesis 21:22-34 and make sure you mark the key words you marked in previous chapters. Mark *covenant* and its synonyms.

2. Genesis 20:2 tells you that Abimelech is king of Gerar.

 a. On the maps located in the Appendix, find *Gerar*.

b. Also note where Lot's descendants, the Moabites and Ammonites, are located.

c. Now note where, according to Genesis 21, Abimelech and Phicol returned to and where Abraham **sojourned** for many days. The word "Palestine" comes from Philistia. Do you realize that the land promised Abraham and his descendants as an everlasting possession is never called Palestine in the Bible?

Look at the maps again and note what the land God promised Abraham and his descendants encompasses.

3. Add the main event(s) of chapter 21 to your "Genesis 1-25 At A Glance" chart.

4. Finally take a good look at Abraham and Abimelech's covenant[1] with one another. The word "make" is *karath* and means "to cut."

a. What was the reason for this covenant?

b. List what they did when they cut this covenant.

---

[1] There is so much more to learn about covenants and customs connected with them. If you would like to learn more, Kay Arthur has written a book called, Our Covenant God: Learning To Trust Him, published by Waterbrook Press. Precept Ministries International also has a Covenant Precept Upon Precept course which is a favorite of many students. They can be ordered by calling Precept Ministries International at 800-763-8280 or by visiting www.precept.org

c. What did Abraham cann God used after making this covenant?

EL OLAM
"EVERLASTING"
GOD

5. Lastly, take some time to record your new insights about God in your "Journal on God."

In Genesis 21:33, we see the first use of El Olam, the Everlasting God. This is a good place to pause and reflect on the God of Abraham, the **Everlasting**, never-changing God, and His Son who longs to call you friend through the New Covenant.

As you near the end of our study of Abraham, the friend of God, examine yourself to make sure that you are "of the seed of Abraham" through faith in the blood of the New Covenant... the blood of Jesus Christ, the Lamb of God who takes away the sins of the world.

How does it all become reality? By faith; not by Law. The Law can only show you your sin; it cannot save you. Salvation comes only through the New Covenant cut at Mount Calvary.

This is why Jesus said, "No longer do I call you slaves, for the slave does not know what his master is doing; but I have called you friends, for all things that I have heard from My Father I have made known to you. You did not choose me, but I chose you, and appointed you that you should go and bear fruit, and that your fruit should remain, so that whatever you ask of the Father in My name, He may give to you" (John 15:15-16).

ENRICHMENT WORDS:

Allegory – the expression by means of symbolic fictional figures and actions of truths or generalizations about human existence.

El Olam – Everlasting God.

Everlasting – lasting or enduring through all time; eternal.

Salvation – deliverance from the power and effects of sin.

Sojourn – to stay as a temporary resident.

Theological – relating to the study of God and His relation to the world.

UNIT SIX

PRECEPT
UPON
PRECEPT®

Abraham
U-6, Chapters 22-25

Journey's End

Abraham... the patriarch of our faith, the friend of God, and a man who struggled in many of the same ways you do. As you think back on all you've learned about him, what have you seen? After every step of faith, Abraham faced a difficult circumstance, suffered a moment of doubt, made a poor choice, but in the end, the writer of Hebrews commends his faith.

His story encourages every believer. Abraham's faith began in response to the miraculous appearance of God. Along the way, God revealed Himself further and Abraham took what he learned and applied it to his life. His faith grew step by step. It's clear this journey of faith was led and authored by God. Now his journey has led him here – to one of the greatest tests of faith ever given to any man!

In this unit you will see how events in Abraham's life culminate in this pivotal moment when his faith is put to the ultimate test. Is he ready? Will he pass? Would you?

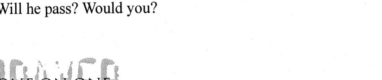

PRAYER ONE ON ONE:

Begin this unit in prayer for your study. Don't let your study be a duty, task, or cold, academic examination of the text. Put yourself in Abraham's place. Abraham faith was being tested to the core. He lived, loved, ached, and grew weary. He experienced battles just like you. Ask God to take you deep into the text to see yourself facing this ultimate sacrifice.

LESSON ONE

In this unit you will encounter an amazing story of sacrifice and love. Most likely you are familiar with this event from childhood stories.

1. Observe and meditate on Genesis 22. Mark the words from your key word bookmark. It is truly an awesome chapter, a mother lode of spiritual riches you'll want to mine carefully so you don't miss one gem of truth.

    As you observe this chapter, you will discover three words that appear in Genesis for the first time: *love*, *worship*, and *obey*. Note their setting and mark each of them in a distinctive way. You'll want to mark these consistently throughout your Bible. If you're keeping a list of key words, add these, plus *covenant*, to that list.

> **Love** – strong affection for another arising out of kinship or personal ties.
>
> **Worship** – to bow down, prostrate oneself before a superior in homage.[1]
>
> **Obey** – to hear, listen to, give heed.[1]

2. Continue to examine the text of Genesis 22 very carefully in the light of the 5 Ws and an H. Don't relax just yet!

Get all the details you can so that you know things like the following: where Abraham went, why, what he did, what happened, how God dealt with him, and how he responded to God.

See if you can find Isaac's at this point. You may need to read further in Genesis.

Record everything you want to remember on the Observation Worksheet.

---

[1]Strong, J. 1996. *The exhaustive concordance of the Bible : Showing every word of the test of the common English version of the canonical books, and every occurence of each word in regular order.* (electronic ed.) . Woodside Bible Fellowship.: Ontario.

Don't panic at the number of assignments you have today; they're not difficult.

1. Today we will look at Hebrews 11:8-19, the "hall of faith" passage, to see what God tells you about Abraham. You looked at Hebrews 11:11 last week; however, there is far more to see. The text is printed below. Look for key words and mark the text as you read it.

    You will get some awesome insights from this chapter that will not only give you a deeper appreciation for Father Abraham but will also cause you to walk in faith.

HEBREWS 11:8-19

8   By faith Abraham, when he was called, obeyed by going out to a place which he was to receive for an inheritance; and he went out, not knowing where he was going.

9   By faith he lived as an alien in the land of promise, as in a foreign *land*, dwelling in tents with Isaac and Jacob, fellow heirs of the same promise;

10 for he was looking for the city which has foundations, whose architect and builder is God.

11 By faith even Sarah herself received ability to conceive, even beyond the proper time of life, since she considered Him faithful who had promised.

12 Therefore there was born even of one man, and him as good as dead at that, *as many descendants* AS THE STARS OF HEAVEN IN NUMBER, AND INNUMERABLE AS THE SAND WHICH IS BY THE SEASHORE.

13 All these died in faith, without receiving the promises, but having seen them and having welcomed them from a distance, and having confessed that they were strangers and exiles on the earth.

14 For those who say such things make it clear that they are seeking a country of their own.

15 And indeed if they had been thinking of that *country* from which they went out, they would have had opportunity to return.

16 But as it is, they desire a better *country*, that is, a heavenly one. Therefore God is not ashamed to be called their God; for He has prepared a city for them.

17 By faith Abraham, when he was tested, offered up Isaac, and he who had received the promises was offering up his only begotten *son*;

18 *it was he* to whom it was said, "IN ISAAC YOUR DESCENDANTS SHALL BE CALLED."

19 He considered that God is able to raise *people* even from the dead, from which he also received him back as a type.

2. According to Hebrews 11:17-19, what did Abraham know? What did he believe God could do if he offered Isaac? You need to see the depth of Abraham's faith – his confidence in the promises of God. As you consider this passage, remember all you have learned about God's promise to Abraham about his descendants.

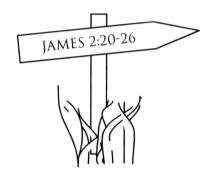

3.   Now look at the following verses in James.

a.   Read these verses, note their context, and then think about how this passage correlates with Genesis 22:12. What did the angel of the Lord say about Abraham in light of what you saw in James?

b. How is Abraham referred to in this passage? Record it below.

> Isn't it amazing to watch God weave truth together! Do you realize how blessed you are to be living on this side of Calvary, to have the whole Word of God... the complete revelation of truth... and your resident tutor, the Holy Spirit, to lead you and guide you into all truth? Doesn't it just make you long to understand every book of the Bible?
>
> Take time now to thank God for giving you access to the truth. Realize how blessed you are, live accordingly, and know that to whom much is given, much is required. Pray that God makes you a faithful steward of His mysteries in the Old and New testaments.

LESSON THREE

JEHOVAH JIREH "THE LORD WILL PROVIDE"

1. When you completed your Observation Worksheet on Genesis 22, did you notice the word *provide* and any synonyms? Re-read the text and mark this key word. Then list below what you learn. Note everything associated with this provision.

> In Genesis 22, Abraham refers to another name of God, YHWH-jireh, "The LORD Will Provide." Today, we refer to God as Jehovah Jireh. Jehovah is an English pronunciation of YHWH with vowels added.

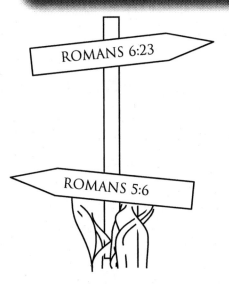

> Later the temple was built on Mount Moriah and sacrifices were made there. The mount runs through Jerusalem. Keep this and events from Genesis 22 in mind as you work through the following questions.

ROMANS 6:23

ROMANS 5:6

2. Look at Genesis 22:2 and note where God told Abraham to make the sacrifice.

a. What sacrifice did God provide in Isaac's place?

b. Read Romans 6:23 and write out what you deserve as payment for your sin.

c. What sacrifice did God provide in *your* place according to Romans 5:6?

MATTHEW 27:33-35

d. Where was this sacrifice slain?

e. What city did this take place in?

Do you see a connection between this sacrifice and the one described in Genesis 22? It's awesome to think about when you see the whole picture. "Take now your son, your only son, whom you love... and offer him there as a burnt offering..." Take a break to reflect on this today – there is more to see in the next lesson.

1. Although the Levitical sacrifices had not yet been instituted at the time of Genesis 22, they were in the heart and mind of God. Read Leviticus 1 and mark every occurrence of *burnt offering*.

> A burnt offering was a **voluntary** offering – it was not required by law.

2. Answer the following to identify main points.

   a. Describe the animal to be offered.

   b. What was the offering for? (1:4) Look at the definition of this word in your Enrichment Words.

   c. What was to be done with the sacrifice?

3. In light of what you learned in Leviticus, what was God asking Abraham to do to Isaac?

4. How is Jesus like Isaac and the burnt offering?

5. Based on what you have seen in this unit alone, what have you learned about God?

    a. How do you know that God loves you?

    b. Is there proof of His love? Look at the following verses. Do you see any comparison between these verses and anything in Genesis 22?

JOHN 3:16-17

6. If you worshiped God now, what would you say to Him in light of what you observed this week? Write it below.

God told Abraham to do a hard thing – to sacrifice his only son, whom he loved. Remember, God's promises to Abraham were to be fulfilled through this son. God was testing him and Abraham passed with flying colors! Nothing was more important to Abraham than obedience.

But this wasn't only a test for Abraham, it was also a demonstration to Abraham, Isaac, and all who would read their story of how God would sacrifice His own Son. It was a picture of how all the families of the earth will one day be blessed through Abraham, when his descendent, Jesus Christ, is sent to earth to voluntarily offer His life as a sacrifice for all mankind.

LESSON FIVE

1.   Read your Observation Worksheet on Genesis 23 and mark the text using your key word bookmark.

2.   Note where Sarah is buried.

3.   Finally, Sarah is cited as an example in 1 Peter. Look up this passage in your Bible and list what you learn about her, why she is cited as an example, and what can be learned from her.

1 PETER 3:1-6

HEBRON PROJECT

WHAT'S YOUR WORLD VIEW?

For this project you will need:

Internet access

What conflicts have occurred in Hebron in modern times? Type "Hebron conflict" in to your preferred search engine. Try to find information that will answer this question. Then print and read the article.

Think about what have you learned in your study of Abraham and this portion of Genesis about Hebron. Who does Hebron belong to? Write a brief summary of the article and determine whether or not the author of the article holds a biblical world-view.

1. You will skip Genesis 24 since this chapter belongs to the study of Isaac. You'll finish this course with Genesis 25:1-18 because it concludes the life of the friend of God. Read this segment of Genesis 25 and note what God tells you about Abraham and his sons, Isaac and Ishmael.

2. Record the following information on "Abraham's Family Tree" in the Appendix:

   a. Abraham's marriage to Keturah, the names of their sons, and their sons' sons (remember God's word to Abraham in Genesis 17:4-6)

   b. Abraham's age at death

   c. Ishmael's sons, and Ishmael's age at death (remember Genesis 17:20)

3. Now compare Abraham's age at his death with his forefathers'. This information is on the chart, "The Overlapping of The Patriarch's Lives," located in the Appendix.

   a. How do Abraham's and Ishmael's ages compare with the ages of the patriarchs who lived before the Flood?

   b. How do the lifespans of Abraham and his contemporaries compare with the average age of men today?

4. Finally, look up the following cross-references and note how Abraham is remembered by his descendants. Note their contexts. Observe who is speaking and the circumstances in which Abraham is mentioned. Record your insights below.

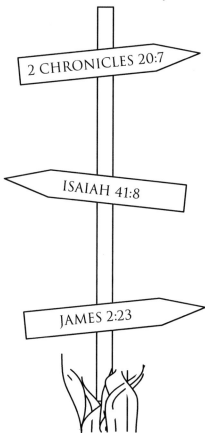

5. Complete your "Genesis 1-25 At A Glance" chart by adding the main events of chapters 22, 23, and 25.

6. Record what you learned about God in your "Journal on God." Take a few minutes to review what you've recorded in your journal during the course. Ask God to reveal Himself to you so you will know Him.

Remember, you too can be Abraham's offspring through Jesus Christ, the Mediator of the New Covenant. All you have to do is to come to God by passing through the rent veil of the flesh of the Son of God. He is the way, the truth, and the life – the only way, for there is salvation in none other than this seed of Abraham.

If you have not made that decision of faith, today can be the day. Tell God that you want to become His child, a follower of the Lord Jesus Christ, and that you are ready to deny yourself, take up your cross, and follow Him for the remainder of your life... that you want, like Abraham, to be God's friend through the New Covenant. Remember...

"Greater love has no one than this, that one lay down his life for his friends. You are My friends if you do what I command you. No longer do I call you slaves, for the slave does not know what his master is doing; but I have called you friends, for all things that I have heard from My Father I have made known to you. You did not choose Me but I chose you, and appointed you that you would go and bear fruit, and that your fruit would remain, so that whatever you ask of the Father in My name He may give to you" (John 15:13-16).

If you continue in His Word, you are truly Jesus' disciple according to John 8:31. This is the mark of a genuine follower of the Lord. Christianity is a life to be lived!

ENRICHMENT WORDS:

Atonement – to cover over sin, make reconciliation.[1]

Love – strong affection for another arising out of kinship or personal ties.

Obey – to hear, listen to, give heed.[1]

Voluntary – proceeding from the will or from one's own choice or consent; implies freedom and spontaneity of choice or action without external compulsion.

Worship – to bow down, prostrate oneself before superior in homage.[1]

---

[1] Strong, J. 1996. *The exhaustive concordance of the Bible : Showing every word of the test of the common English version of the canonical books, and every occurence of each word in regular order.* (electronic ed.) . Woodside Bible Fellowship.: Ontario

APPENDIX

CONTENTS:

· GENESIS 11-25 OBSERVATION WORKSHEETS

· GENESIS 1-25 AT A GLANCE CHART

· ABRAHAM'S JOURNEY CHAPTERS 11-14 MAPS

· ABRAHAM'S FAMILY TREE

· THE PATRIARCH'S LIVES CHART

· A PROFILE ON LOT CHART

· MY JOURNAL ON GOD

· ABOUT PRECEPT MINISTRIES INTERNATIONAL

GENESIS 11:24-32
Observation Worksheet

Chapter Theme _____

24   Nahor lived twenty-nine years, and became the father of Terah;

25   and Nahor lived one hundred and nineteen years after he became the father of Terah, and he had *other* sons and daughters.

26   Terah lived seventy years, and became the father of Abram, Nahor and Haran.

27   Now these are *the records of* the generations of Terah. Terah became the father of Abram, Nahor and Haran; and Haran became the father of Lot.

28   Haran died in the presence of his father Terah in the land of his birth, in Ur of the Chaldeans.

29   Abram and Nahor took wives for themselves. The name of Abram's wife was Sarai; and the name of Nahor's wife was Milcah, the daughter of Haran, the father of Milcah and Iscah.

30   Sarai was barren; she had no child.

31   Terah took Abram his son, and Lot the son of Haran, his grandson, and Sarai his daughter-in-law, his son Abram's wife; and they went out together from Ur of the Chaldeans in order to enter the land of Canaan; and they went as far as Haran, and settled there.

32   The days of Terah were two hundred and five years; and Terah died in Haran.

GENESIS 12
Observation Worksheet

Chapter Theme _____

NOW the LORD said to Abram,

"Go forth from your country,

And from your relatives

And from your father's house,

To the land which I will show you;

2   And I will make you a great nation,

And I will bless you,

And make your name great;

And so you shall be a blessing;

3   And I will bless those who bless you,

And the one who curses you I will curse.

And in you all the families of the earth will be blessed."

4   So Abram went forth as the LORD had spoken to him; and Lot went with him. Now Abram was seventy-five years old when he departed from Haran.

5   Abram took Sarai his wife and Lot his nephew, and all their possessions which they had accumulated, and the persons which they had acquired in Haran, and they set out for the land of Canaan; thus they came to the land of Canaan.

6   Abram passed through the land as far as the site of Shechem, to the oak of Moreh. Now the Canaanite *was* then in the land.

7   The LORD appeared to Abram and said, "To your descendants I will give this land." So he built an altar there to the LORD who had appeared to him.

8   Then he proceeded from there to the mountain on the east of Bethel, and pitched his tent, with Bethel on the west and Ai on the east; and there he built an altar to the LORD and called upon the name of the LORD.

9   Abram journeyed on, continuing toward the Negev.

10   Now there was a famine in the land; so Abram went down to Egypt to sojourn

there, for the famine was severe in the land.

11　It came about when he came near to Egypt, that he said to Sarai his wife, "See now, I know that you are a beautiful woman;

12　and when the Egyptians see you, they will say, 'This is his wife'; and they will kill me, but they will let you live.

13　"Please say that you are my sister so that it may go well with me because of you, and that I may live on account of you."

14　It came about when Abram came into Egypt, the Egyptians saw that the woman was very beautiful.

15　Pharaoh's officials saw her and praised her to Pharaoh; and the woman was taken into Pharaoh's house.

16　Therefore he treated Abram well for her sake; and gave him sheep and oxen and donkeys and male and female servants and female donkeys and camels.

17　But the LORD struck Pharaoh and his house with great plagues because of Sarai, Abram's wife.

18　Then Pharaoh called Abram and said, "What is this you have done to me? Why did you not tell me that she was your wife?

19　"Why did you say, 'She is my sister,' so that I took her for my wife? Now then, here is your wife, take her and go."

20　Pharaoh commanded *his* men concerning him; and they escorted him away, with his wife and all that belonged to him.

GENESIS 13
Observation Worksheet

Chapter Theme _____

SO Abram went up from Egypt to the Negev, he and his wife and all that belonged to him, and Lot with him.

2 Now Abram was very rich in livestock, in silver and in gold.

3 He went on his journeys from the Negev as far as Bethel, to the place where his tent had been at the beginning, between Bethel and Ai,

4 to the place of the altar which he had made there formerly; and there Abram called on the name of the LORD.

5 Now Lot, who went with Abram, also had flocks and herds and tents.

6 And the land could not sustain them while dwelling together, for their possessions were so great that they were not able to remain together.

7 And there was strife between the herdsmen of Abram's livestock and the herdsmen of Lot's livestock. Now the Canaanite and the Perizzite were dwelling then in the land.

8 So Abram said to Lot, "Please let there be no strife between you and me, nor between my herdsmen and your herdsmen, for we are brothers.

9 "Is not the whole land before you? Please separate from me; if *to* the left, then I will go to the right; or if *to* the right, then I will go to the left."

10 Lot lifted up his eyes and saw all the valley of the Jordan, that it was well watered everywhere—*this was* before the LORD destroyed Sodom and Gomorrah—like the garden of the LORD, like the land of Egypt as you go to Zoar.

11 So Lot chose for himself all the valley of the Jordan, and Lot journeyed eastward. Thus they separated from each other.

12 Abram settled in the land of Canaan, while Lot settled in the cities of the valley, and moved his tents as far as Sodom.

13 Now the men of Sodom were wicked exceedingly and sinners against the LORD.

14 The LORD said to Abram, after Lot had separated from him, "Now lift up your eyes and look from the place where you are, northward and southward and eastward and westward;

15 for all the land which you see, I will give it to you and to your descendants forever.

16 "I will make your descendants as the dust of the earth, so that if anyone can number the dust of the earth, then your descendants can also be numbered.

17 "Arise, walk about the land through its length and breadth; for I will give it to you."

18 Then Abram moved his tent and came and dwelt by the oaks of Mamre, which are in Hebron, and there he built an altar to the LORD.

GENESIS 14
Observation Worksheet

Chapter Theme _____

AND it came about in the days of Amraphel king of Shinar, Arioch king of Ellasar, Chedorlaomer king of Elam, and Tidal king of Goiim,

2   *that* they made war with Bera king of Sodom, and with Birsha king of Gomorrah, Shinab king of Admah, and Shemeber king of Zeboiim, and the king of Bela (that is, Zoar).

3   All these came as allies to the valley of Siddim (that is, the Salt Sea).

4   Twelve years they had served Chedorlaomer, but the thirteenth year they rebelled.

5   In the fourteenth year Chedorlaomer and the kings that were with him, came and defeated the Rephaim in Ashteroth-karnaim and the Zuzim in Ham and the Emim in Shaveh-kiriathaim,

6   and the Horites in their Mount Seir, as far as El-paran, which is by the wilderness.

7   Then they turned back and came to En-mishpat (that is, Kadesh), and conquered all the country of the Amalekites, and also the Amorites, who lived in Hazazon-tamar.

8   And the king of Sodom and the king of Gomorrah and the king of Admah and the king of Zeboiim and the king of Bela (that is, Zoar) came out; and they arrayed for battle against them in the valley of Siddim,

9   against Chedorlaomer king of Elam and Tidal king of Goiim and Amraphel king of Shinar and Arioch king of Ellasar—four kings against five.

10   Now the valley of Siddim was full of tar pits; and the kings of Sodom and Gomorrah fled, and they fell into them. But those who survived fled to the hill country.

11   Then they took all the goods of Sodom and Gomorrah and all their food supply,

and departed.

12 They also took Lot, Abram's nephew, and his possessions and departed, for he was living in Sodom.

13 Then a fugitive came and told Abram the Hebrew. Now he was living by the oaks of Mamre the Amorite, brother of Eshcol and brother of Aner, and these were allies with Abram.

14 When Abram heard that his relative had been taken captive, he led out his trained men, born in his house, three hundred and eighteen, and went in pursuit as far as Dan.

15 He divided his forces against them by night, he and his servants, and defeated them, and pursued them as far as Hobah, which is north of Damascus.

16 He brought back all the goods, and also brought back his relative Lot with his possessions, and also the women, and the people.

17 Then after his return from the defeat of Chedorlaomer and the kings who were with him, the king of Sodom went out to meet him at the valley of Shaveh (that is, the King's Valley).

18 And Melchizedek king of Salem brought out bread and wine; now he was a priest of God Most High.

19 He blessed him and said,

"Blessed be Abram of God Most High,

Possessor of heaven and earth;

20 And blessed be God Most High,

Who has delivered your enemies into your hand."

He gave him a tenth of all.

21 The king of Sodom said to Abram, "Give the people to me and take the goods for yourself."

22 Abram said to the king of Sodom, "I have sworn to the LORD God Most High, possessor of heaven and earth,

23 that I will not take a thread or a sandal thong or anything that is yours, for fear you would say, 'I have made Abram rich.'

24   "I will take nothing except what the young men have eaten, and the share of the men who went with me, Aner, Eshcol, and Mamre; let them take their share."

GENESIS 15
Observation Worksheet

Chapter Theme _____

AFTER these things the word of the Lord came to Abram in a vision, saying,

"Do not fear, Abram,

I am a shield to you;

Your reward shall be very great."

2 Abram said, "O Lord God, what will You give me, since I am childless, and the heir of my house is Eliezer of Damascus?"

3 And Abram said, "Since You have given no offspring to me, one born in my house is my heir."

4 Then behold, the word of the Lord came to him, saying, "This man will not be your heir; but one who will come forth from your own body, he shall be your heir."

5 And He took him outside and said, "Now look toward the heavens, and count the stars, if you are able to count them." And He said to him, "So shall your descendants be."

6 Then he believed in the Lord; and He reckoned it to him as righteousness.

7 And He said to him, "I am the Lord who brought you out of Ur of the Chaldeans, to give you this land to possess it."

8 He said, "O Lord God, how may I know that I will possess it?"

9 So He said to him, "Bring Me a three year old heifer, and a three year old female goat, and a three year old ram, and a turtledove, and a young pigeon."

10 Then he brought all these to Him and cut them in two, and laid each half opposite the other; but he did not cut the birds.

11 The birds of prey came down upon the carcasses, and Abram drove them away.

12 Now when the sun was going down, a deep sleep fell upon Abram; and behold, terror *and* great darkness fell upon him.

13   *God* said to Abram, "Know for certain that your descendants will be strangers in a land that is not theirs, where they will be enslaved and oppressed four hundred years.

14   "But I will also judge the nation whom they will serve, and afterward they will come out with many possessions.

15   "As for you, you shall go to your fathers in peace; you will be buried at a good old age.

16   "Then in the fourth generation they will return here, for the iniquity of the Amorite is not yet complete."

17   It came about when the sun had set, that it was very dark, and behold, *there appeared* a smoking oven and a flaming torch which passed between these pieces.

18   On that day the LORD made a covenant with Abram, saying,

"To your descendants I have given this land,

From the river of Egypt as far as the great river, the river Euphrates:

19   the Kenite and the Kenizzite and the Kadmonite

20   and the Hittite and the Perizzite and the Rephaim

21   and the Amorite and the Canaanite and the Girgashite and the Jebusite."

GENESIS 16
Observation Worksheet

Chapter Theme _____

NOW Sarai, Abram's wife had borne him no *children*, and she had an Egyptian maid whose name was Hagar.

2 So Sarai said to Abram, "Now behold, the LORD has prevented me from bearing *children*. Please go in to my maid; perhaps I will obtain children through her." And Abram listened to the voice of Sarai.

3 After Abram had lived ten years in the land of Canaan, Abram's wife Sarai took Hagar the Egyptian, her maid, and gave her to her husband Abram as his wife.

4 He went in to Hagar, and she conceived; and when she saw that she had conceived, her mistress was despised in her sight.

5 And Sarai said to Abram, "May the wrong done me be upon you. I gave my maid into your arms, but when she saw that she had conceived, I was despised in her sight. May the Lord judge between you and me."

6 But Abram said to Sarai, "Behold, your maid is in your power; do to her what is good in your sight." So Sarai treated her harshly, and she fled from her presence.

7 Now the angel of the LORD found her by a spring of water in the wilderness, by the spring on the way to Shur.

8 He said, "Hagar, Sarai's maid, where have you come from and where are you going?" And she said, "I am fleeing from the presence of my mistress Sarai."

9 Then the angel of the LORD said to her, "Return to your mistress, and submit yourself to her authority."

10 Moreover, the angel of the LORD said to her, "I will greatly multiply your descendants so that they will be too many to count."

11 The angel of the LORD said to her further,

"Behold, you are with child,

And you will bear a son;

And you shall call his name Ishmael,

Because the LORD has given heed to your affliction.

12   "He will be a wild donkey of a man,

        His hand *will be* against everyone,

        And everyone's hand *will be* against him;

        And he will live to the east of all his brothers."

13   Then she called the name of the LORD who spoke to her, "You are a God who sees"; for she said, "Have I even remained alive here after seeing Him?"

14   Therefore the well was called Beer-lahai-roi; behold, it is between Kadesh and Bered.

15 So Hagar bore Abram a son; and Abram called the name of his son, whom Hagar bore, Ishmael.

16   Abram was eighty-six years old when Hagar bore Ishmael to him.

GENESIS 17
Observation Worksheet

Chapter Theme _____

NOW when Abram was ninety-nine years old, the LORD appeared to Abram and said to him,

"I am God Almighty;

Walk before Me, and be blameless.

2   "I will establish My covenant between Me and you,

And I will multiply you exceedingly."

3   Abram fell on his face, and God talked with him, saying,

4   "As for Me, behold, My covenant is with you,

And you will be the father of a multitude of nations.

5   "No longer shall your name be called Abram,

But your name shall be Abraham;

For I will make you the father of a multitude of nations.

6   "I will make you exceedingly fruitful, and I will make nations of you, and kings will come forth from you.

7   "I will establish My covenant between Me and you and your descendants after you throughout their generations for an everlasting covenant, to be God to you and to your descendants after you.

8   "I will give to you and to your descendants after you, the land of your sojournings, all the land of Canaan, for an everlasting possession; and I will be their God."

9   God said further to Abraham, "Now as for you, you shall keep My covenant, you and your descendants after you throughout their generations.

10   "This is My covenant, which you shall keep, between Me and you and your descendants after you: every male among you shall be circumcised.

11   "And you shall be circumcised in the flesh of your foreskin, and it shall be the

sign of the covenant between Me and you.

12   "And every male among you who is eight days old shall be circumcised throughout your generations, a *servant* who is born in the house or who is bought with money from any foreigner, who is not of your descendants.

13   "A *servant* who is born in your house or who is bought with your money shall surely be circumcised; thus shall My covenant be in your flesh for an everlasting covenant.

14   "But an uncircumcised male who is not circumcised in the flesh of his foreskin, that person shall be cut off from his people; he has broken My covenant."

15   Then God said to Abraham, "As for Sarai your wife, you shall not call her name Sarai, but Sarah *shall be* her name.

16   "I will bless her, and indeed I will give you a son by her. Then I will bless her, and she shall be *a mother of* nations; kings of peoples will come from her."

17   Then Abraham fell on his face and laughed, and said in his heart, "Will a child be born to a man one hundred years old? And will Sarah, who is ninety years old, bear *a child*?"

18   And Abraham said to God, "Oh that Ishmael might live before You!"

19   But God said, "No, but Sarah your wife will bear you a son, and you shall call his name Isaac; and I will establish My covenant with him for an everlasting covenant for his descendants after him.

20   "As for Ishmael, I have heard you; behold, I will bless him, and will make him fruitful and will multiply him exceedingly. He shall become the father of twelve princes, and I will make him a great nation.

21   "But My covenant I will establish with Isaac, whom Sarah will bear to you at this season next year."

22   When He finished talking with him, God went up from Abraham.

23   Then Abraham took Ishmael his son, and all *the servants* who were born in his house and all who were bought with his money, every male among the men of Abraham's household, and circumcised the flesh of their foreskin in the very same day, as God had said to him.

24 Now Abraham was ninety-nine years old when he was circumcised in the flesh of his foreskin.

25 And Ishmael his son was thirteen years old when he was circumcised in the flesh of his foreskin.

26 In the very same day Abraham was circumcised, and Ishmael his son.

27 All the men of his household, who were born in the house or bought with money from a foreigner, were circumcised with him.

GENESIS 18
Observation Worksheet

Chapter Theme _____

NOW the Lord appeared to him by the oaks of Mamre, while he was sitting at the tent door in the heat of the day.

2   When he lifted up his eyes and looked, behold, three men were standing opposite him; and when he saw *them*, he ran from the tent door to meet them and bowed himself to the earth,

3   and said, "My lord, if now I have found favor in your sight, please do not pass your servant by.

4   "Please let a little water be brought and wash your feet, and rest yourselves under the tree;

5   and I will bring a piece of bread, that you may refresh yourselves; after that you may go on, since you have visited your servant." And they said, "So do, as you have said."

6   So Abraham hurried into the tent to Sarah, and said, "Quickly, prepare three measures of fine flour, knead *it* and make bread cakes."

7   Abraham also ran to the herd, and took a tender and choice calf and gave *it* to the servant, and he hurried to prepare it.

8   He took curds and milk and the calf which he had prepared, and placed *it* before them; and he was standing by them under the tree as they ate.

9   Then they said to him, "Where is Sarah your wife?" And he said, "There, in the tent."

10   He said, "I will surely return to you at this time next year; and behold, Sarah your wife will have a son." And Sarah was listening at the tent door, which was behind him.

11   Now Abraham and Sarah were old, advanced in age; Sarah was past childbear-

ing.

12 Sarah laughed to herself, saying, "After I have become old, shall I have pleasure, my lord being old also?"

13 And the LORD said to Abraham, "Why did Sarah laugh, saying, 'Shall I indeed bear *a child*, when I am *so* old?'

14 "Is anything too difficult for the LORD? At the appointed time I will return to you, at this time next year, and Sarah will have a son."

15 Sarah denied *it* however, saying, "I did not laugh"; for she was afraid. And He said, "No, but you did laugh."

16 Then the men rose up from there, and looked down toward Sodom; and Abraham was walking with them to send them off.

17 The LORD said, "Shall I hide from Abraham what I am about to do,

18 since Abraham will surely become a great and mighty nation, and in him all the nations of the earth will be blessed?

19 "For I have chosen him, so that he may command his children and his household after him to keep the way of the LORD by doing righteousness and justice, so that the LORD may bring upon Abraham what He has spoken about him."

20 And the LORD said, "The outcry of Sodom and Gomorrah is indeed great, and their sin is exceedingly grave.

21 "I will go down now, and see if they have done entirely according to its outcry, which has come to Me; and if not, I will know."

22 Then the men turned away from there and went toward Sodom, while Abraham was still standing before the LORD.

23 Abraham came near and said, "Will You indeed sweep away the righteous with the wicked?

24 "Suppose there are fifty righteous within the city; will You indeed sweep *it* away and not spare the place for the sake of the fifty righteous who are in it?

25 "Far be it from You to do such a thing, to slay the righteous with the wicked, so that the righteous and the wicked are *treated* alike. Far be it from You! Shall not

the Judge of all the earth deal justly?"

26   So the L<small>ORD</small> said, "If I find in Sodom fifty righteous within the city, then I will spare the whole place on their account."

27   And Abraham replied, "Now behold, I have ventured to speak to the Lord, although I am *but* dust and ashes.

28   "Suppose the fifty righteous are lacking five, will You destroy the whole city because of five?" And He said, "I will not destroy *it* if I find forty-five there."

29   He spoke to Him yet again and said, "Suppose forty are found there?" And He said, "I will not do *it* on account of the forty."

30   Then he said, "Oh may the Lord not be angry, and I shall speak; suppose thirty are found there?" And He said, "I will not do *it* if I find thirty there."

31   And he said, "Now behold, I have ventured to speak to the Lord; suppose twenty are found there?" And He said, "I will not destroy *it* on account of the twenty."

32   Then he said, "Oh may the Lord not be angry, and I shall speak only this once; suppose ten are found there?" And He said, "I will not destroy *it* on account of the ten."

33   As soon as He had finished speaking to Abraham the L<small>ORD</small> departed, and Abraham returned to his place.

GENESIS 19
Observation Worksheet

Chapter Theme _____

NOW the two angels came to Sodom in the evening as Lot was sitting in the gate of Sodom. When Lot saw *them*, he rose to meet them and bowed down *with his* face to the ground.

2   And he said, "Now behold, my lords, please turn aside into your servant's house, and spend the night, and wash your feet; then you may rise early and go on your way." They said however, "No, but we shall spend the night in the square."

3   Yet he urged them strongly, so they turned aside to him and entered his house; and he prepared a feast for them, and baked unleavened bread, and they ate.

4   Before they lay down, the men of the city, the men of Sodom, surrounded the house, both young and old, all the people from every quarter;

5   and they called to Lot and said to him, "Where are the men who came to you tonight? Bring them out to us that we may have relations with them."

6   But Lot went out to them at the doorway, and shut the door behind him,

7   and said, "Please, my brothers, do not act wickedly.

8   "Now behold, I have two daughters who have not had relations with man; please let me bring them out to you, and do to them whatever you like; only do nothing to these men, inasmuch as they have come under the shelter of my roof."

9   But they said, "Stand aside." Furthermore, they said, "This one came in as an alien, and already he is acting like a judge; now we will treat you worse than them." So they pressed hard against Lot and came near to break the door.

10 But the men reached out their hands and brought Lot into the house with them, and shut the door.

11 They struck the men who were at the doorway of the house with blindness, both small and great, so that they wearied *themselves trying* to find the doorway.

12 Then the *two* men said to Lot, "Whom else have you here? A son-in-law, and your sons, and your daughters, and whomever you have in the city, bring *them* out of the place;

13   for we are about to destroy this place, because their outcry has become so great before the Lᴏʀᴅ that the Lᴏʀᴅ has sent us to destroy it."

14   Lot went out and spoke to his sons-in-law, who were to marry his daughters, and said, "Up, get out of this place, for the Lᴏʀᴅ will destroy the city." But he appeared to his sons-in-law to be jesting.

15   When morning dawned, the angels urged Lot, saying, "Up, take your wife and your two daughters who are here, or you will be swept away in the punishment of the city."

16   But he hesitated. So the men seized his hand and the hand of his wife and the hands of his two daughters, for the compassion of the Lᴏʀᴅ *was* upon him; and they brought him out, and put him outside the city.

17   When they had brought them outside, one said, "Escape for your life! Do not look behind you, and do not stay anywhere in the valley; escape to the mountains, or you will be swept away."

18   But Lot said to them, "Oh no, my lords!

19   "Now behold, your servant has found favor in your sight, and you have magnified your lovingkindness, which you have shown me by saving my life; but I cannot escape to the mountains, for the disaster will overtake me and I will die;

20   now behold, this town is near *enough* to flee to, and it is small. Please, let me escape there (is it not small?) that my life may be saved."

21   He said to him, "Behold, I grant you this request also, not to overthrow the town of which you have spoken.

22   "Hurry, escape there, for I cannot do anything until you arrive there." Therefore the name of the town was called Zoar.

23   The sun had risen over the earth when Lot came to Zoar.

24   Then the Lᴏʀᴅ rained on Sodom and Gomorrah brimstone and fire from the Lᴏʀᴅ out of heaven,

25   and He overthrew those cities, and all the valley, and all the inhabitants of the cities, and what grew on the ground.

26   But his wife, from behind him, looked *back*, and she became a pillar of salt.

27   Now Abraham arose early in the morning *and went* to the place where he had stood before the Lord;

28   and he looked down toward Sodom and Gomorrah, and toward all the land of the valley, and he saw, and behold, the smoke of the land ascended like the smoke of a furnace.

29   Thus it came about, when God destroyed the cities of the valley, that God remembered Abraham, and sent Lot out of the midst of the overthrow, when He overthrew the cities in which Lot lived.

30   Lot went up from Zoar, and stayed in the mountains, and his two daughters with him; for he was afraid to stay in Zoar; and he stayed in a cave, he and his two daughters.

31   Then the firstborn said to the younger, "Our father is old, and there is not a man on earth to come in to us after the manner of the earth.

32   "Come, let us make our father drink wine, and let us lie with him that we may preserve our family through our father."

33   So they made their father drink wine that night, and the firstborn went in and lay with her father; and he did not know when she lay down or when she arose.

34   On the following day, the firstborn said to the younger, "Behold, I lay last night with my father; let us make him drink wine tonight also; then you go in and lie with him, that we may preserve our family through our father."

35   So they made their father drink wine that night also, and the younger arose and lay with him; and he did not know when she lay down or when she arose.

36   Thus both the daughters of Lot were with child by their father.

37   The firstborn bore a son, and called his name Moab; he is the father of the Moabites to this day.

38   As for the younger, she also bore a son, and called his name Ben-ammi; he is the father of the sons of Ammon to this day.

GENESIS 20
Observation Worksheet

Chapter Theme _____

NOW Abraham journeyed from there toward the land of the Negev, and settled between Kadesh and Shur; then he sojourned in Gerar.

2   Abraham said of Sarah his wife, "She is my sister." So Abimelech king of Gerar sent and took Sarah.

3   But God came to Abimelech in a dream of the night, and said to him, "Behold, you are a dead man because of the woman whom you have taken, for she is married."

4   Now Abimelech had not come near her; and he said, "Lord, will You slay a nation, even *though* blameless?

5   "Did he not himself say to me, 'She is my sister'? And she herself said, 'He is my brother.' In the integrity of my heart and the innocence of my hands I have done this."

6   Then God said to him in the dream, "Yes, I know that in the integrity of your heart you have done this, and I also kept you from sinning against Me; therefore I did not let you touch her.

7   "Now therefore, restore the man's wife, for he is a prophet, and he will pray for you and you will live. But if you do not restore *her*, know that you shall surely die, you and all who are yours."

8   So Abimelech arose early in the morning and called all his servants and told all these things in their hearing; and the men were greatly frightened.

9   Then Abimelech called Abraham and said to him, "What have you done to us? And how have I sinned against you, that you have brought on me and on my kingdom a great sin? You have done to me things that ought not to be done."

10   And Abimelech said to Abraham, "What have you encountered, that you have done this thing?"

11   Abraham said, "Because I thought, surely there is no fear of God in this place, and they will kill me because of my wife.

12   "Besides, she actually is my sister, the daughter of my father, but not the daugh-

ter of my mother, and she became my wife;

13 and it came about, when God caused me to wander from my father's house, that I said to her, 'This is the kindness which you will show to me: everywhere we go, say of me, "He is my brother." ' "

14 Abimelech then took sheep and oxen and male and female servants, and gave them to Abraham, and restored his wife Sarah to him.

15 Abimelech said, "Behold, my land is before you; settle wherever you please."

16 To Sarah he said, "Behold, I have given your brother a thousand pieces of silver; behold, it is your vindication before all who are with you, and before all men you are cleared."

17 Abraham prayed to God, and God healed Abimelech and his wife and his maids, so that they bore *children*.

18 For the LORD had closed fast all the wombs of the household of Abimelech because of Sarah, Abraham's wife.

GENESIS 21
Observation Worksheet

Chapter Theme _____

THEN the LORD took note of Sarah as He had said, and the LORD did for Sarah as He had promised.

2   So Sarah conceived and bore a son to Abraham in his old age, at the appointed time of which God had spoken to him.

3   Abraham called the name of his son who was born to him, whom Sarah bore to him, Isaac.

4   Then Abraham circumcised his son Isaac when he was eight days old, as God had commanded him.

5   Now Abraham was one hundred years old when his son Isaac was born to him.

6   Sarah said, "God has made laughter for me; everyone who hears will laugh with me."

7   And she said, "Who would have said to Abraham that Sarah would nurse children? Yet I have borne him a son in his old age."

8   The child grew and was weaned, and Abraham made a great feast on the day that Isaac was weaned.

9   Now Sarah saw the son of Hagar the Egyptian, whom she had borne to Abraham, mocking.

10   Therefore she said to Abraham, "Drive out this maid and her son, for the son of this maid shall not be an heir with my son Isaac."

11   The matter distressed Abraham greatly because of his son.

12   But God said to Abraham, "Do not be distressed because of the lad and your maid; whatever Sarah tells you, listen to her, for through Isaac your descendants shall be named.

13   "And of the son of the maid I will make a nation also, because he is your descendant."

14   So Abraham rose early in the morning and took bread and a skin of water and gave *them* to Hagar, putting *them* on her shoulder, and *gave her* the boy, and sent her

away. And she departed and wandered about in the wilderness of Beersheba.

15 When the water in the skin was used up, she left the boy under one of the bushes.

16 Then she went and sat down opposite him, about a bowshot away, for she said, "Do not let me see the boy die." And she sat opposite him, and lifted up her voice and wept.

17 God heard the lad crying; and the angel of God called to Hagar from heaven and said to her, "What is the matter with you, Hagar? Do not fear, for God has heard the voice of the lad where he is.

18 "Arise, lift up the lad, and hold him by the hand, for I will make a great nation of him."

19 Then God opened her eyes and she saw a well of water; and she went and filled the skin with water and gave the lad a drink.

20 God was with the lad, and he grew; and he lived in the wilderness and became an archer.

21 He lived in the wilderness of Paran, and his mother took a wife for him from the land of Egypt.

22 Now it came about at that time that Abimelech and Phicol, the commander of his army, spoke to Abraham, saying, "God is with you in all that you do;

23 now therefore, swear to me here by God that you will not deal falsely with me or with my offspring or with my posterity, but according to the kindness that I have shown to you, you shall show to me and to the land in which you have sojourned."

24 Abraham said, "I swear it."

25 But Abraham complained to Abimelech because of the well of water which the servants of Abimelech had seized.

26 And Abimelech said, "I do not know who has done this thing; you did not tell me, nor did I hear of it until today."

27 Abraham took sheep and oxen and gave them to Abimelech, and the two of them made a covenant.

28 Then Abraham set seven ewe lambs of the flock by themselves.

29 Abimelech said to Abraham, "What do these seven ewe lambs mean, which you have set by themselves?"

30 He said, "You shall take these seven ewe lambs from my hand so that it may be a witness to me, that I dug this well."

31 Therefore he called that place Beersheba, because there the two of them took an oath.

32 So they made a covenant at Beersheba; and Abimelech and Phicol, the commander of his army, arose and returned to the land of the Philistines.

33 *Abraham* planted a tamarisk tree at Beersheba, and there he called on the name of the Lord, the Everlasting God.

34 And Abraham sojourned in the land of the Philistines for many days.

GENESIS 22
Observation Worksheet

Chapter Theme _____

NOW it came about after these things, that God tested Abraham, and said to him, "Abraham!" And he said, "Here I am."

2   He said, "Take now your son, your only son, whom you love, Isaac, and go to the land of Moriah, and offer him there as a burnt offering on one of the mountains of which I will tell you."

3   So Abraham rose early in the morning and saddled his donkey, and took two of his young men with him and Isaac his son; and he split wood for the burnt offering, and arose and went to the place of which God had told him.

4   On the third day Abraham raised his eyes and saw the place from a distance.

5   Abraham said to his young men, "Stay here with the donkey, and I and the lad will go over there; and we will worship and return to you."

6   Abraham took the wood of the burnt offering and laid it on Isaac his son, and he took in his hand the fire and the knife. So the two of them walked on together.

7   Isaac spoke to Abraham his father and said, "My father!" And he said, "Here I am, my son." And he said, "Behold, the fire and the wood, but where is the lamb for the burnt offering?"

8   Abraham said, "God will provide for Himself the lamb for the burnt offering, my son." So the two of them walked on together.

9   Then they came to the place of which God had told him; and Abraham built the altar there and arranged the wood, and bound his son Isaac and laid him on the altar, on top of the wood.

10   Abraham stretched out his hand and took the knife to slay his son.

11   But the angel of the LORD called to him from heaven and said, "Abraham, Abraham!" And he said, "Here I am."

12   He said, "Do not stretch out your hand against the lad, and do nothing to him; for now I know that you fear God, since you have not withheld your son, your only son, from Me."

13 Then Abraham raised his eyes and looked, and behold, behind *him* a ram caught in the thicket by his horns; and Abraham went and took the ram and offered him up for a burnt offering in the place of his son.

14 Abraham called the name of that place The LORD Will Provide, as it is said to this day, "In the mount of the LORD it will be provided."

15 Then the angel of the LORD called to Abraham a second time from heaven,

16 and said, "By Myself I have sworn, declares the LORD, because you have done this thing and have not withheld your son, your only son,

17 indeed I will greatly bless you, and I will greatly multiply your seed as the stars of the heavens and as the sand which is on the seashore; and your seed shall possess the gate of their enemies.

18 "In your seed all the nations of the earth shall be blessed, because you have obeyed My voice."

19 So Abraham returned to his young men, and they arose and went together to Beersheba; and Abraham lived at Beersheba.

20 Now it came about after these things, that it was told Abraham, saying, "Behold, Milcah also has borne children to your brother Nahor:

21 Uz his firstborn and Buz his brother and Kemuel the father of Aram

22 and Chesed and Hazo and Pildash and Jidlaph and Bethuel."

23 Bethuel became the father of Rebekah; these eight Milcah bore to Nahor, Abraham's brother.

24 His concubine, whose name was Reumah, also bore Tebah and Gaham and Tahash and Maacah.

GENESIS 23
Observation Worksheet

Chapter Theme _____

NOW Sarah lived one hundred and twenty-seven years; *these were* the years of the
life of Sarah.

2   Sarah died in Kiriath-arba (that is, Hebron) in the land of Canaan; and Abraham went
in to mourn for Sarah and to weep for her.

3   Then Abraham rose from before his dead, and spoke to the sons of Heth, saying,

4   "I am a stranger and a sojourner among you; give me a burial site among you that I
may bury my dead out of my sight."

5   The sons of Heth answered Abraham, saying to him,

6   "Hear us, my lord, you are a mighty prince among us; bury your dead in the choicest
of our graves; none of us will refuse you his grave for burying your dead."

7   So Abraham rose and bowed to the people of the land, the sons of Heth.

8   And he spoke with them, saying, "If it is your wish *for me* to bury my dead out of my
sight, hear me, and approach Ephron the son of Zohar for me,

9   that he may give me the cave of Machpelah which he owns, which is at the end of his
field; for the full price let him give it to me in your presence for a burial site."

10   Now Ephron was sitting among the sons of Heth; and Ephron the Hittite answered Abraham in the hearing of the sons of Heth; *even* of all who went in at
the gate of his city, saying,

11   "No, my lord, hear me; I give you the field, and I give you the cave that is in it.
In the presence of the sons of my people I give it to you; bury your dead."

12   And Abraham bowed before the people of the land.

13   He spoke to Ephron in the hearing of the people of the land, saying, "If you will
only please listen to me; I will give the price of the field, accept *it* from me that
I may bury my dead there."

14   Then Ephron answered Abraham, saying to him,

15   "My lord, listen to me; a piece of land worth four hundred shekels of silver, what
is that between me and you? So bury your dead."

16   Abraham listened to Ephron; and Abraham weighed out for Ephron the silver which he had named in the hearing of the sons of Heth, four hundred shekels of silver, commercial standard.

17   So Ephron's field, which was in Machpelah, which faced Mamre, the field and cave which was in it, and all the trees which were in the field, that were within all the confines of its border, were deeded over

18   to Abraham for a possession in the presence of the sons of Heth, before all who went in at the gate of his city.

19   After this, Abraham buried Sarah his wife in the cave of the field at Machpelah facing Mamre (that is, Hebron) in the land of Canaan.

20   So the field and the cave that is in it, were deeded over to Abraham for a burial site by the sons of Heth.

GENESIS 25:1-18
Observation Worksheet

Chapter Theme _____

NOW Abraham took another wife, whose name was Keturah.

2   She bore to him Zimran and Jokshan and Medan and Midian and Ishbak and Shuah.

3   Jokshan became the father of Sheba and Dedan. And the sons of Dedan were Asshurim and Letushim and Leummim.

4   The sons of Midian *were* Ephah and Epher and Hanoch and Abida and Eldaah. All these *were* the sons of Keturah.

5   Now Abraham gave all that he had to Isaac;

6   but to the sons of his concubines, Abraham gave gifts while he was still living, and sent them away from his son Isaac eastward, to the land of the east.

7   These are all the years of Abraham's life that he lived, one hundred and seventy-five years.

8   Abraham breathed his last and died in a ripe old age, an old man and satisfied *with life*; and he was gathered to his people.

9   Then his sons Isaac and Ishmael buried him in the cave of Machpelah, in the field of Ephron the son of Zohar the Hittite, facing Mamre,

10   the field which Abraham purchased from the sons of Heth; there Abraham was buried with Sarah his wife.

11   It came about after the death of Abraham, that God blessed his son Isaac; and Isaac lived by Beer-lahai-roi.

12   Now these are *the records of* the generations of Ishmael, Abraham's son, whom Hagar the Egyptian, Sarah's maid, bore to Abraham;

13   and these are the names of the sons of Ishmael, by their names, in the order of their birth: Nebaioth, the firstborn of Ishmael, and Kedar and Adbeel and Mibsam

14   and Mishma and Dumah and Massa,

15 Hadad and Tema, Jetur, Naphish and Kedemah.

16 These are the sons of Ishmael and these are their names, by their villages, and by their camps; twelve princes according to their tribes.

17 These are the years of the life of Ishmael, one hundred and thirty-seven years; and he breathed his last and died, and was gathered to his people.

18 They settled from Havilah to Shur which is east of Egypt as one goes toward Assyria; he settled in defiance of all his relatives.

AT A GLANCE CHART

Abraham
Genesis 1-25 At A Glance

BOOK THEME:

KEY WORDS & PHRASES:

CHAPTER THEMES:

1	Creation in Six Days
2	Creation of Mankind
3	The Fall
4	Cain and Abel
5	Life under the Curse
6	Setting for the Flood Judgment
7	The Flood
8	The End of the Flood
9	God's Covenant with Noah
10	Nations Separated after the Flood
11	
12	
13	
14	
15	
16	
17	
18	
19	
20	
21	
22	
23	
24	
25	

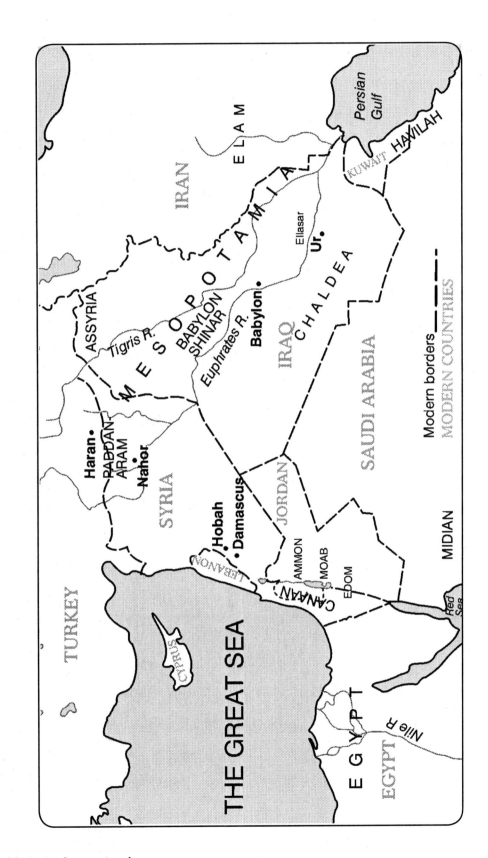

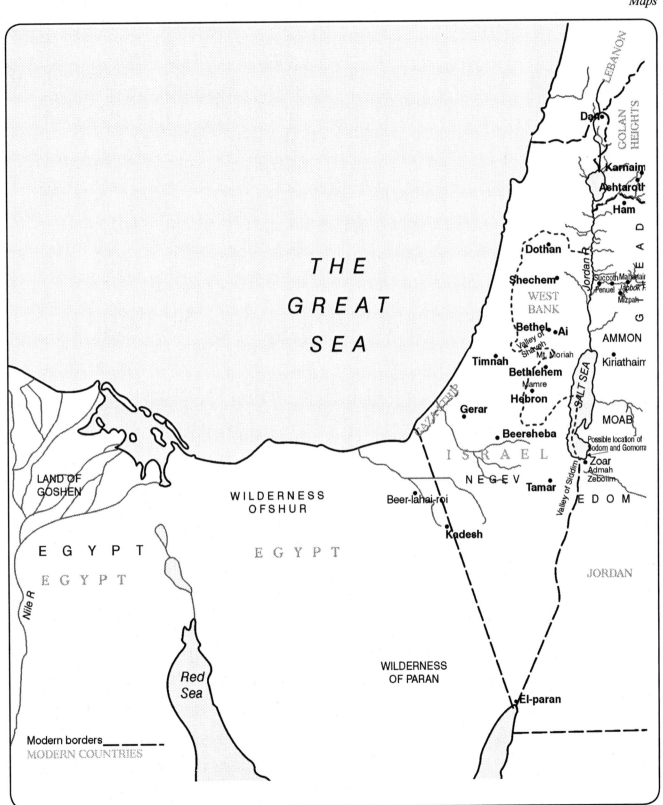

PRECEPT
UPON
PRECEPT®

ABRAHAM'S FAMILY TREE

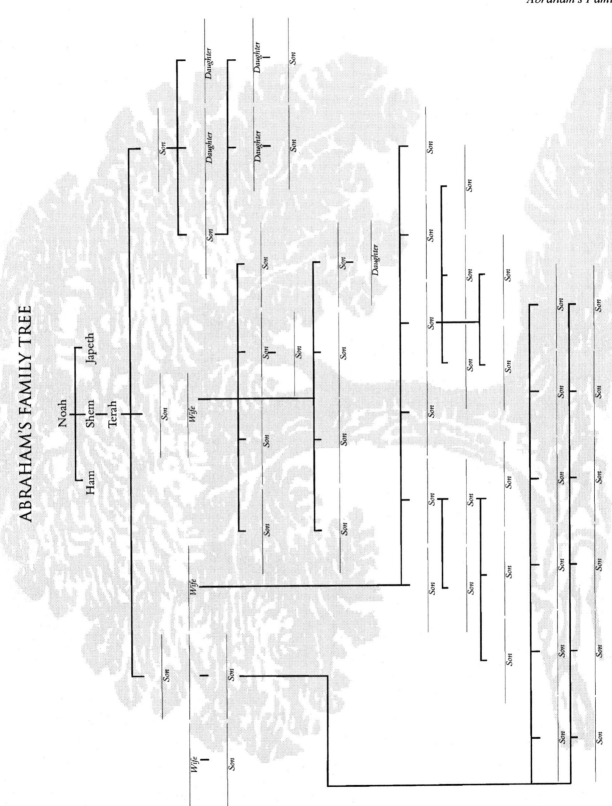

Noah

Ham
Shem
Japeth

Terah

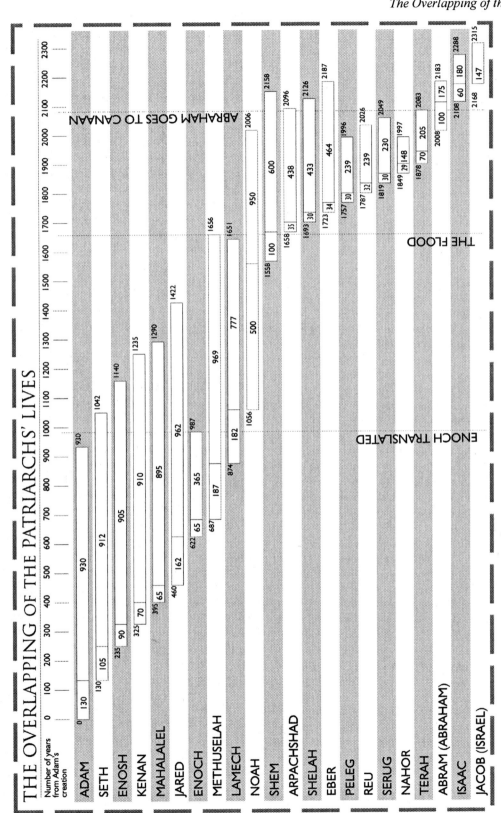

THE OVERLAPPING OF THE PATRIARCHS' LIVES

KEY: The first number inside the block is the man's age when his son (whose name is in the next line below) was born. The second number in the block is the number of years the man lived. The numbers preceding and following each block are the number of years from Adam's creation.

A PROFILE ON LOT

JOURNAL ON GOD

Abraham